We the Body—Christ the Head

We the Body—Christ the Head

Dr. Carol Cash

iUniverse, Inc.
New York Lincoln Shanghai

We the Body—Christ the Head

iUniverse books may be ordered through booksellers or by contacting:

iUniverse
2021 Pine Lake Road, Suite 100
Lincoln, NE 68512
www.iuniverse.com
1-800-Authors (1-800-288-4677)

ISBN: 0-595-35055-0

Printed in the United States of America

This is For You

I wish to thank my family for all the support they have given me while doing this project. They have been there through all the tears and self doubts. Gene, for believing in me. Tony and Joe for just calling to say, "I love you." And in the order of ages, Jaimie, Heather, Brittany, Amber, Callie, Todd, Paige, and Alex for the way their eyes twinkled when I announced the writing of this book and the many, "You go, Nanny!" responses they made. To Dianne and Lisa, our daughters-in-law for listening and doing the things you do that made it possible to add to the contents and show there are still spiritual marriages today.

Many thanks go to Rev. Cynthia Lovingood and her valued input. I appreciate you, lady, more than you'll ever know.

To Phil Whitmarsh at iUniverse who didn't forget my name after the first time we spoke on the phone. He has aided me tirelessly and was such a joy. Thank you, Phil, for not loosing patience with me. You definitely have the fruit of the Spirit in temperance.

Undying gratitude goes to all our troops. You are the Rambos. You are the Chuck Norris' of this world and I thank God for you. Without you, people like me could not continue spreading the Word and being an Ambassador for Christ. But most of all, I thank your families for the unselfish love that let you fight for our freedom.

May God eternally bless you all.

Contents

Forward

When Dr. Cash asked me to read the manuscript We the Body—Christ the Head she was writing I was honored, but at the same time concerned about how much time I could spend in reading anything else with my busy schedule. She faxed me the first few pages and I found some quiet time and the first page caught my interest. From that point on, I could not wait to come in from work, find my quiet time and sit down to read some more. On one occasion I even asked her when she would be sending some more pages for me to read. Once you start reading the book I believe you will feel the same way.

Dr. Cash's personality is seen throughout this book and will draw you into one great message. Her unique way of comparing the physical body with the spiritual body is just something you need to read for yourself. I believe she will capture your heart in her writing just as she has mine.

There is a little humor in her writing, as you will see. As you read the book and if you will be honest with yourself, you will be able to see a little bit of you in the physical sense and understand how the spiritual you, should be working. Her message can change your life for the better. She gives Scriptures to back up all she is telling you so you can know that she is not just pulling things out of a hat because it sounds good.

So, grab your coffee, or in my case a diet Pepsi, sit back and open up this wonderful message on '*We the Body—Christ the Head*'. I pray you will open your heart to receive that which the Lord has for you in this message.

Rev. Cynthia Lovingood

Introduction

The body of man is the earthly house of the soul and spirit of man. The soul and spirit design, and the body executes. The human body as the heavens is a wonderful creation.

The body contains:

263 bones

600 muscles

970 miles of blood vessels

30 pounds or 6 quarts of blood

and there are 32 feet of intestines.

All your blood makes a complete circle in your body every two minutes. The heart is a pump about 4 by 6 inches in size and beats about 70 times a minute. At each beat 4 ounces of blood is expelled from the heart. This means that your heart pumps approximately 12 tons of blood a day. This is an equal force of lifting 20 tons a foot high.

You breathe about 2400 gallons of air a day.

The brain of a man weighs about 3 pounds and 2 ounces. The brain of a woman weighs about 2 pounds and 12 ounces. There are about 10 million nerves all of which are connected to the spinal column.

Each square inch of skin contains 3500 sweating tubes.

The nose can smell about 6000 different odors while the ear can distinguish every known sound by the use of 20,000 tuning hairs in the ear.

A 200-pound body of a man contains:

¼ ounce of iron

1/5 ounce of sugar

2 ounces of salt

24 pounds of coal in carbon form

10 gallons of water

1/10 of a drop of iodine

2 pounds of phosphorus

112 cubic feet of oxygen

50 cubic feet of nitrogen

56 pounds of hydrogen and

7 pounds of lime
making a total value of the human body approximately 98 cents.

Author Unknown

1

In the Beginning

"Will it hurt if I hit it with a hammer?"

"No, but it would break the bones."

I was four and my cousin, a grown man, had come to visit us. I did not understand the words 'stroke' and 'paralyzed'. All I knew was that he walked with a cane, dragging his left leg. His left hand and arm hung lifeless at his side. When he needed to move it, he would reach with his right hand and put his left in the desired position.

This was amazing to me. I mean my left arm moved any time it wanted to. I didn't even have to tell it to pick up my crayons. Actually, my arm really listened to my mother. When she said, "Pick up you toys," my left arm would do as it was told. And of course, it listened to my mother more than me, because it never tried to pick up the toys without her saying so.

So what was his problem? I knew if my left arm did not listen to my mother there would be some serious consequences that usually resulted in unwanted pain on a place somewhere below my left arm and slightly to the right. So through the eyes of a four year old, I wondered if he had pain or was about to experience it. Being told it would break the bones left my imagination running wild.

Time moved on and so did we; to another state, another school, another job, another place to find new friends. And my vision of an unruly arm soon left me.

My next encounter of the confusing kind was when I was about ten. My father was an alcoholic and there had been times when he was taken to the doctor or an emergency room. The alcohol controlled him so much that he was eventually committed to a rehab program where he underwent psychological evaluation. The letter my mother received from the psychologist only proved what my mother thought, but left me more confused than ever. According to her, he said they could find nothing to substantiate his behavior except he was just mean. All his problems were in his head. Of course, this was years ago when addiction was still a sin, not a disease. By the way, when did it become fashionable to buy a disease in a bottle?

This didn't make sense either. There were no cuts, no bruises and no drainage of any kind. He had hair, two eyes, two ears, a nose and a mouth...with teeth. He spoke, he walked, he ate, he slept and he worked. Well, sometimes he worked. I could not envision a head in a place where man's head was not intended to be, throwing up the same food he had just proclaimed was delicious. Whatever problems he had in his head, I surely didn't want any of them.

◆   ◆   ◆

I was sixteen and it was Saturday night. I worked part time slinging hamburgers on a grill and had just gotten home. My brother had joined the Marines and was waiting to leave. He had a date with a beautiful girl that would later become his wife. It was around 11:00 PM and an officer was knocking on the door. He informed us they had been in an accident and were in a local hospital. When we arrived at the medical center we found that his girlfriend was in surgery with some critical injuries. My brother's head was bandaged considerably and he was very drowsy. He had suffered some head wounds but nothing that would not heal. Although he was in pain, he could go home. That was a relief but the Marines didn't think so. Because of it being a head wound, he was refused entry. Upon re-evaluation it proved he did not have much feeling in his forehead. This would eventually come back but they still turned him down. This was during the Vietnam conflict and he didn't want to get drafted into the army, so he ended up joining the Navy. The injuries weren't sufficient to keep him out of service, just out of the Marines. He was very disappointed.

However, that just confirmed to me his head injuries were a lot worse than the doctors thought. I mean what person in his right mind would want to join an outfit where the likelihood of getting killed was very high? And to show disappointment at not being allowed in had to prove there was brain damage. I decided right then to one day understand people's line of thinking and what made their bodies respond as they do. I would be almost twenty-five before I learned we actually function under a form of mind control by two powers, but we do have the free will to decide which power will control us.

◆   ◆   ◆

Many other events would surface in my life to make me ask endless questions. And sometimes the endless questions would only make me wonder what was in my head to make me ask endless questions. That scared me! I knew I was getting on people's nerve (or was that just in my head?) when a preacher told me I needed to stop asking so many questions and listen to him. That aroused anger because I have a hard enough time listening to my husband without trying to listen to a pen-headed theologian that can't give me scriptures to explain my questions.

Of course, my anger erupted, not in a lame arm or loss of feeling (my feelings were quite obvious) but through my tongue. Then I really had concerns because my tongue didn't listen to me like my left arm would listen to my mother. It just kept running like a commode with faulty plumbing.

Then I reached a point where I enjoyed taunting people, you know, playing mind games. I thrilled at watching their expressions when I asked questions or made statements that would make their topic of conversation sound ludicrous. Most people speak before they put the tongue in gear. It's like when the phone rings at three in the morning and the person on the other end says something very intelligent like, "Did I wake you?"

"No," you reply. "I had to get up to answer the phone anyway."

And why do people always have to comment on the obvious? I love it when our sons call and when I answer the phone they say, "Oh, are you home?"

"No," I reply. "This is a timed release response on the answering machine. You are speaking to a pre-recorded message."

Several times my husband has reprimanded me when we would attend some function. Just as we would be exiting the car, he would smile, point his finger in my face (his finger always obeys him) and warn me, "Now be nice." I found this quite annoying, as I am always nice. If you don't believe it just ask me.

One day I got tired of it all. Let's face it. I wasn't getting anywhere and my best friend in the whole world had yelled at me to stop analyzing everything. (Hi, Ann. I told you I'd get even with you for yelling at me and now your name is plastered all over a book. So there!)

Now what *she* did wasn't nice but she got my attention. Yes, sir. I had another question. Why would she yell at me and my husband smile when they both were reprimanding me for the same thing? Why did she find my actions infuriating and he would find them funny?

By this time I had learned that the brain controlled every thing we do. If there is a problem in the way we responded, or the way we see things, then it had to begin there, or get messed up in the translation before we acted on the command. Although I still hadn't figured out why my left arm would listen to my mother more than me, except when my brain conveyed the message that my mother had spoken to my arm. This was still confusing because my arm doesn't have ears.

Actually, I might be able to understand. During my college years I learned we sometimes respond by association. And this is good because it works. I know it works because my arm would associate pain in another location if it did not follow her wishes.

Ahhh. Association. One of the most powerful words in the human language. Webster defines it this way: the act of being associated. (Oh, boy—here's your sign.)

With WHAT?

Combination, relationship, an organization of persons having a common interest: society, something linked in memory or imagination with a thing or person. The process of forming mental connections or bonds between sensations. Now I know why my arm responded to my mother. It formed a mental connection with a sensation…pain.

After my friend yelled at me I decided to do a little research. Of course, in doing research one must ask a lot of questions and that was right up my alley. But at least now I had a purpose…a legitimate purpose. Now I could go to people who understand the brain, or at least portions of it, and ask all the questions I wanted. But in doing this I was constantly left with the unanswered question of why?

It was then I went to the one I should have gone to in the first place. The One Who made the brain. That made sense. After all, if you want to know how to make a cake do you go to a mechanic? Of course not, although I have eaten some that tasted that way. And if a mechanic wants to learn about a particular car he usually goes to the manual that is written by the designer.

God designed our brain and our body. Some people think we evolved after a big bang and the earth was formed. This may be true, because the big bang could have come when Satan was cast out of Heaven. He must have collided with something hard. I guess that would have been God's foot as He placed it ever so firmly on Satan's backside. Sounds reasonable to me. You know if God's voice can sound like thunder, just think what an impact His foot would make when force was exerted from His leg where the foot is attached.

In His Word, Jesus often used illustrations to explain His point. Israel was an agricultural nation so He often used parables of planting and harvesting. Paul, however, in I Corinthians 12, used a different illustration to help them understand.

Corinth was an important cosmopolitan city located in the Roman province of Achaia (the southern part of modern-day Greece) on a large isthmus about fifty miles west of Athens. Situated along a major trade route it had a thriving economy. Numbers of sailors and merchants from every nation flocked to the city and during the first century it was one of the richest.

For this reason it was a strategic center of influence for the gospel and the travelers there could carry it to all parts of the world. Now, we know every nation was not strictly agricultural and other illustrations were needed. Paul, as led by the inspiration of the Holy Ghost, used the example of the body.

One thing that really stands out in this passage is how no one part of the body can say that it has no need of another part. Kind of puts all the different denominations in their place doesn't it? Right now there is so much arguing in the Body it literally makes me sick. I think we have more spiritual murders than we do physical ones. It's no wonder we can no longer see new converts or churches filled to capacity.

When we first moved to the state we are now in, the first thing we did was start asking about a place to worship. I remember one time in particular we were in a restaurant and the waitress began to speak of our Lord. This impressed us and of course we started exchanging experiences of our Christian walk. She sounded so close to God and so knowledgeable that we ask her where she went to worship. She explained that she didn't get to attend very often because of her work. This I could understand but it sidestepped the question. This should have given us our first clue.

However, she finally went on to tell us her father was the pastor and he had been in the ministry for forty-two years. He was so strong and a great example for her. She spoke of healings and commitments within the church with strong dedications and the people's desire to learn. She spoke of her father's ability to discern spiritual influences with the flock and her mother's deep-rooted knowledge of the Word. By this time, we were so interested we thought maybe God was revealing that we should look no longer. We had found the place. So with great anticipation we slid to the edge of our seats and asked, "How large is you dad's church?"

Smiling she replied, "He usually runs around eighteen or nineteen. And he's never taken a penny for his services."

Simultaneously my husband and I glanced at each other and I could see his shoulders sag. "What is wrong with this picture?" our eyes spoke silently to each other.

OK. Let's look at it. The Bible says in Matthew 10:10 that, "…for the workman is worthy of his meat." The local church is supposed to take care of their pastor. If he *sooo* humbly does not accept, he is not following the Lord's direction and in reality, he is ever *sooo* humbly denying his flock of a blessing.

The Bible also says in Mark 16:15 for us to go into all the world and preach the gospel to every creature. Now I ask you, how can God bless and increase the church if a pastor of forty-two years hasn't' taken the full benefits of being a leader and a child of God. I truly feel if a church is not growing, something is wrong in the Body.

I've seen so many people that believe the old saying about a pastor. You know, "Lord You keep him humble and we'll keep him poor." And a lot of times they will follow it with, "Salvation is free so I don't believe in paying a preacher." This is not biblical at all. God paid a handsome price for our salvation. And the least we can do is provide a way for someone to tell others full time.

Other comments bother me such as, "Oh, we've been here for twelve years. Yep, we have good dedicated people. My son (or son-in-law, both of which may be the ripe old age of twenty) is my associate pastor. My wife (or daughter) plays the piano…by ear of course. You know, we're not professionals and we sing by letter. We just open our mouth and letter fly. Ha, ha, ha. My aunt teaches the little fellas. She's one hundred and fifty years old but she's like that watch. You know the kind. She takes a lickin' and keeps on tickin'. Some of our services are so spiritual we've actually had people swing from the chandeliers. Yes, sirreeee, been here twelve years and already running twenty people if they're not all working."

Don't misunderstand me. I see nothing wrong with your family being your associate. There is nothing wrong with playing an instrument 'by ear'. I do myself. There is nothing wrong with a small attendance or getting emotional. However…

After twelve years, if the Body hasn't reproduced any more cells or at least grown to a nice healthy number forty, something is wrong. Somewhere along the line the Body has forgotten the depth of Calvary and is neglecting to reproduce. Calvary was not some office picnic and the Body needs a broader picture of what happened. The Body needs to have it seared into the heart.

My son emailed me a description of the crucifixion as told by a medical doctor.

Let me take the time to retell it and please…try to remember, it should have been us.

◆　　　◆　　　◆

What Is a Crucifixion?

The cross is placed on the ground and the exhausted man is quickly thrown backwards with his shoulders against the wood. The legionnaire feels for the depression at the front of the wrist. He drives a heavy, square, wrought nail through the wrist deep into the wood. Quickly he moves to the other side and repeats the action, being careful not to pull the arms too tightly, but allow some flexing and movement.

The cross is then lifted into place. The left foot is pressed backward against the right foot, and with both feet extended, toes down, a nail is driven through the arch of each, leaving the knees flexed.

The victim is now crucified. As he slowly sags down with more weight on the nails in the wrist, excruciating fiery pain shoots along the fingers and up the arms to explode in the brain. The nails in the wrist are putting pressure on the median nerves. As he pushes himself upward to avoid this stretching torment, he places the full weight on the nails through his feet.

Again he feels the searing agony of the nail tearing through the nerves between the bones of his feet. As the arms fatigue, cramps sweep through the muscles, knotting them with deep relentless, throbbing pain. Air can be drawn into the lungs, but not exhaled. He fights to raise himself in order to get even one small breath. Finally, carbon dioxide builds up in the lungs and in the blood stream, and the cramps partially subside. Spasmodically, he is able to push himself upward to exhale and bring in life giving oxygen. Hours of limitless pain, cycles of twisting, joint wrenching cramps, intermittent partial asphyxiation, searing pain as tissue is torn from his lacerated back as he moves up and down against the rough timber.

Then another agony begins: a deep crunching pain deep in the chest as the pericardium slowly fills with serum and begins to compress the heart. It is almost over, the loss of tissue fluids has reached a critical level: the compressed heart is struggling to pump heavy, thick sluggish blood into the tissues, the tortured lungs are making frantic efforts to gasp in small gulps of air. He can feel the chill of death creeping through his tissues. Finally, he can allow his body to die. All of this, and the Bible records it with the simple words, "And the crucified Him." Mark 15:24

◆   ◆   ◆

I've spoken in a lot of churches, and do you know what I hear more than anything? It's the digs against our brothers and sisters of a different belief. Everyone thinks his denomination is the only one going to heaven. They are the only ones that are right. They forget that we are the ones that should have been crucified and instead of trying to reach others, they ride their hobbyhorse and are perfectly content to be blissfully ignorant. So before I end this chapter, allow me to quote the infamous President Richard Nixon in saying, "Let me make this perfectly clear."

There are some things in the faith you cannot debate, deny or denounce in order for us to call each other brother or sister. Personally, I know of five fundamentals of the faith and if someone claims salvation through Jesus Christ our Lord but denies any of these five, I'm afraid I cannot worship with that person in Spirit and in Truth. These five are:

One: The Bible is the infallible inspired Word of God. There can be no argument or doubts over this. It is quite plain in II Timothy 3:16 that says all Scripture is given by inspiration of God. It is profitable for doctrine, reproof, correction and instruction in righteousness. And guess what? In writing this Paul is actually speaking of the Old Testament because the New Testament didn't exist at that time. Paul thought he was only writing a letter of instruction and encouragement to the young preacher. He had no way of knowing his literature would one day be a compilation of many of the other letters he had written or would write. So please understand, he emphatically meant the Torah. The upcoming generation usually ask the question, "How do we know God inspired men to write the Bible?"

It's really elementary, my dear Watson. All you have to do is really study it and it becomes quite obvious. For instance, our great hero Columbus sailed across the ocean in search of spices. Personally, I go to Walmart, but that's beside the point. His upcoming trip was a source of fear for some because everyone thought the world was flat and they could just picture good ole' Chris going off the deep end. Now if Chris, a self-professed Christian, had been studying the Word, he would have found in Isaiah 40:22 that God sits upon the circle of the earth.

Also, it took over forty men a period of 1600 years to write the Bible. They all had one subject, one purpose. The ones writing what we call the Old Testament wrote concerning a Perfect Sacrifice and they were looking toward the cross. The ones writing the New Testament wrote concerning a Perfect Sacrifice and they were looking back to the cross. This perfect Sacrifice was one Person, Jesus Christ. And what makes it so amazing is most of these men didn't even know each other and I'm sure that Isaiah, Jeremiah, and Ezekiel weren't faxing each other their sermon notes nor pulling up any prize winning papers on the internet.

Most of all, this Book has survived over the years. Men have tried to destroy it, tried to analyze it, tried to disgrace and belittle it. So far, they have lost. Why? Again we look to the Bible. Matthew 24:35 says, "Heaven and earth shall pass away, but my words shall not pass away."

Also, years ago the medical world thought if a person got sick, all they had to do was withdraw a little blood. It was called bloodletting. Someone feeling really bad would simply drop by the doctor's office or house and he would remove some blood. The patient would stand up, stretch and say, "Yep, I feel better now. Got rid of all those germs in my blood."

Now we know that's not true. But if they had read the Bible to begin with, they would have known it then because it says in Leviticus 17:14 the life is in the blood. These nuts were removing life instead of taking care of it. These are just a few of the reasons why we must admit and agree the Bible is the Word of God.

Two: Jesus was born of a virgin birth. God promised that a Redeemer would come. Isaiah prophesied of a virgin in chapter seven. All the people who studied the Law and knew of this prophecy still did not believe it when it happened. Why?

Because they didn't think He fit the mold. Kinda like our denominationalism of today, isn't it? Let me emphasize that various differences in the Body effect the way the world sees us and frankly we are painting a very poor picture. For instance, some believe in the necessity of water baptism and some don't. Some believe in once saved always saved, and some don't. . Some believe in speaking in tongues and some don't. Some believe in women being a doormat and some don't. With all of these I say unto you, that Jesus' words in regard to our salvation and being a part of the Body was, "YOU MUST BE BORN AGAIN." Simple.

That's why you must believe in the virgin birth. According to God's Word in Romans 5:12 it plainly states that it was because of one man (that man being Adam) sin entered into the world, and death by sin (we were originally created to physically live forever) and so death passed upon all men for all have sinned.

Now I ask you. How can death pass upon all men just because one man messes up royally? Hang in there with me for a few seconds, OK? I'm trying to prove a point that is causing great illness in the Body. This was all a part of making progress in my search for significance.

Anyway, we are still speaking of the virgin birth. Go back to Genesis 2:18. Now watch this carefully and the order in which it falls. In verse eighteen God decided man should not be alone. And that's true because sometimes a man is dangerous when left alone, like in the kitchen. So God was trying to prove a point, too.

Now look real close at the *next* two verses. In verse nineteen he has used the ground to form every beast of the field and every fowl of the air. *Then* He brings the animals to Adam. That's cool. God knew He had created an intelligent man. Adam had to be intelligent and use his brain to the max because he named all of them in one day. We're so lazy we can't even remember the date of our anniversary. Moving on....

Now drop on down to verse twenty and this is where it gets real good. Adam gave names to all cattle, fowl, and beast and guess what! It plainly says there was *not* found a help meet for him. Now ain't that a blip? It appears that God's first choice, *after* making the statement it was not good for man to be alone, was one of the creatures already created. He made the statement and *then* brought them to Adam. Just think, if Adam had taken a fancy to one of these animals, where would we be?

Our *'mother of living'* could have been a baboon! Or worse yet, a giraffe. What if he had fallen in love with a vulture? But Adam, being the intelligent man that he was, decided the baboon had bad breath, the giraffe was too tall to try to kiss, and the vulture's dietary desire were just a little too much to contend with. By him not finding a mate among all those choices it should make us appreciate the commandment to honor thy father and mother a little more than we do. OK. Let's get back to sin and the virgin birth.

We've established that sin was brought into the world through Adam. When they were first created, Adam and Eve had perfect blood: no flaws, no diabetes, no low hemoglobin...perfect. Since sin came through him thereby rendering sin hereditary, it was vital that the bloodline was pure and so it had to be through a virgin.

The lineage of a person comes from a man and since sin is passed to every man through Adam it was essential that Mary had never known a man. Only pure blood would meet the requirements God demanded for our reconciliation with Him. Therefore, we must believe in a virgin birth. The virgin birth was a sign to the Jews but more than that; it was a necessity for our salvation.

Three: Jesus was the substitute sacrifice for our sins. Our works can't do it, our church membership can't do it, our family name can't do it, our wealth and fame can't do it, our good looks, well, those of you that have good looks, can't do it.

Even how much we know about God's Word won't do it. Don't get mad. It's true. You can know the Bible all you want to, but if you don't know the Author, you won't have a leg to stand on come Judgment Day.

Four: Jesus bodily arose from the dead. "Oh, it's just a spiritual thing," most people say. Use your head, Einstein. If it was just spiritual why did Jesus tell Thomas to thrust his hand into His side? Do you think Thomas would have tried to tickle a spirit? Nope. He arose!

And of course, the fifth fundamental is one of the most important. At least I think so. That fundamental fact is Jesus is returning bodily. The disciples had already accepted the fact that Jesus had risen. They had already accepted the fact that it was bodily. So when He ascended He did it bodily. We find the account of this in Acts 1:10. But the great thing is, in verse 11 the angels proudly proclaimed that He was coming back.

"But that's still just spiritual," some will say. So read the next part of the verse. It tells us He is coming back because the angels said He shall come again in like manner. Get that? LIKE manner. He left bodily and He'll return BODILY.

II Peter 3:4 tells us that in the last days there will be scoffers saying, "…Where is the promise of His coming? For since the fathers fell asleep, all things continue as they were from the beginning of the creation."

It seems I have heard this more and more as the time gets closer, more from the New Agers than anyone. And every time I hear it I want to shout because they do not realize they are taking the stance of a flashing neon sigh that is saying, "Jesus is coming, Jesus is coming, Jesus is coming!"

As long as we agree on these five, I can worship with and call someone brother or sister. But the rest of the things we argue about are literally tearing the Body apart. Can we not realize the Christian Army is the only military that wants to bury its wounded? If one's practice of worship is a little different than ours, we automatically label them wrong. We find it easy to love and worship with those who are good-looking or fun to have around, or who believe exactly the way we do.

We don't like people who inconvenience us or make us feel uncomfortable. We would rather stay away from people who aren't as healthy, pretty or smart as we are. Do we as Baptist, Methodist, Pentecostal, or Lutheran have the monopoly on the proper way of worship? Thankfully, there is someone who won't treat us badly if we do it different. Someone who loves us with an unconditional love that welcomes us into the family forever, regardless of how messed up we are. And that One is the Head.

Based on Christ being the Head, and our heads being a microscopic cell in the Body, I began to wonder about all the portions of the brain and how they represent things in the Bible. Recently while sitting in a pastor's office, he said that while he had been waiting at the doctor's office for his physical, he happened to notice a chart of the brain on the wall. Now, he is as inquisitive and analytical as I am so it wasn't unusual for him to lean back, place his hands behind his head and say, "Now there's a sermon in there somewhere."

There is brother!! So take that ball and run with!

2

We the Body

Many years went by and eventually the Lord managed to crack through my thick skull. I had tried to stop analyzing and be a nice person. What I called playing mind games and trying to get people to think about what they were saying just didn't have as much humor and appeal as it once did. My husband said I was growing up. I preferred to think of it as maturing. Growing up sounds so childish, don't you think?

He knocked on our door on January 3, 1975. He welcomed us to the neighborhood since we had just recently been transferred. After we had shown our southern hospitality, this stranger actually had the nerve to butt into our personal business and ask us if we were to die right then, where would we go.

Now I had watched a lot of *saved* people in my life and wasn't sure I wanted any part of it. When I told him I had tried Jesus but it didn't last, he smiled and said, "Well, stop trying Jesus, and *let* Jesus." This smart alec had the answer for everything.

So much so, he began to make sense. He started to make me feel quite uncomfortable. His topic and patience began to get under my skin. In fact, it got under my skin so far, it wiggled its way into my blood stream and as any first year medical student knows, any thing that is in your blood stream eventually passes through the heart. Notice I said passes *through*.

The trouble was, it didn't pass through. It lodged there. My heart started to beat faster, trying to dislodge this alien being. My pulse was rapid, my breathing labored and shallow, my skin became clammy. Sounds like a heart attack? Of course, it was.

God's convicting power was lodged right there in the right ventricle. I knew without being told it was then or never. Death to this world would have been a welcome relief and I knelt down in our living room and prayed the sinner's prayer. It was 9:27 PM. I remember the time because this precious man wrote it in the front of my Bible.

I didn't know it then, but he was giving me the first tool to use against the devil when he began to tell me I really wasn't saved. Each time that happened I would go back to my Bible and read aloud the time and tell him he was a liar. It took three weeks for me to gain victory over his darts of doubt. You see, I had always thought there must be something special happen…crying, shouting, fireworks, something. But the preacher had said we were saved by faith and not feelings so I had to walk on the naked truth.

This story was told to me as a true incident but I have no way of proving it. It was supposed to have happened a few years ago at a university in the south.

It seems there was a professor of philosophy there who was a deeply committed atheist. His primary goal for one required class was to spend the entire semester attempting to prove that God could not exist. His students were always afraid to argue with him because of his impeccable logic. For twenty years he had taught this class and no one had ever had the courage to go against him. Sure, some had argued in class at times, but no one had ever really gone against him because of his reputation.

At the end of every semester on the last day, he would say to his class of 300 students, "If there is anyone here who still believes in Jesus, stand up!" In twenty years no one had ever stood up. They knew what he was going to do next. He would say, "Because anyone who believes in God is a fool. If God existed, He would stop this piece of chalk from hitting the ground and breaking."

And every year he would drop the chalk onto the tile floor of the classroom and it would shatter into a hundred pieces. All of the students would do nothing but stop and stare. Most of the students thought God couldn't exist. Certainly a number of Christians had slipped through, but for twenty years they had been too afraid to stand up.

A few years ago there was a freshman that happened to enroll. He was a Christian and had heard the stories about his professor. He was required to take the class for his major and he was afraid. But the three months of that semester he prayed every morning that he would have the courage to stand up no matter what the professor said or what the class thought. Nothing they said could ever shatter his faith…he hoped.

Finally the day came. The professor said, "If there is anyone here who still believes in God, stand up!" The professor and 300 students looked at him, shocked as he stood up at the back of the classroom.

The professor shouted, "You fool!!" If God existed, he would keep this piece of chalk from breaking when it hit the ground!"

He proceeded to drop the chalk, but as he did it slipped out of his fingers, off his shirt cuff, onto the pleat of his pants, down his leg and off his shoe. As it hit the ground, it simply rolled away…unbroken.

The professor's jaw dropped as he stared at the chalk. He looked up at the young man and then left the lecture hall. The young man who had stood proceeded to walk to the front of the room and shared his faith in Jesus for the next half hour. 300 students stayed and listened as he told of God's love for them and His power through Jesus.

Walking by faith is hard. Hebrews 11:1 says, "…faith is the substance of things hoped for, the evidence of things not seen."

Substance—the material of which anything consists. Most people will never believe what I am about to write. But it actually happened to about 150 employees.

Payday had arrived. We were still young in our marriage and our home was totally furnished with early yard sale. Nothing matched and we were proud of it. It was our first home that would one day belong to us, instead of the bank. Oh, how we had pinched pennies to buy it. It was hard. Do you have any idea what it's like to not be able to go to McDonald's at least once a week?

My husband worked for a very reputable company that is now international. At the time it would have been the last thing on anyone's mind that the payroll checks were going to bounce. But within a week of paying bills (one of which was our third house payment) employees began to receive notices from the banks with the very nasty words of 'check returned due to insufficient funds."

Now this didn't hurt too many employees because they were older and had built a nice little nest egg. We, on the other hand, had just gone broke making a down payment on a home plus ever so slowly paying off our son's hospital stay of thirty-two days. My husband went ballistic.

"Have you spent any money you've not told me about?" the first suspect (which was me) was questioned.

"No!" came the stung voiced reply.

"Well, *sommme body did!*"

"Well, it wasn't *meee*. And since you carry the checkbook, *whooom* does that leave?" (I can be nasty and sarcastic, too)

Later that day his partner called and said, "Have you gotten the word that our payroll checks bounced? I got a notice from the bank today. Ain't that a fine howdy do?"

He had a little nest egg and *fine howdy do* wasn't exactly what my husband was feeling at the moment.

It was a simply mistake. This company, like most others, had a separate payroll account and someone had messed up royally with the deposit. At least that is what we were told. Hard to believe? You bet. Especially when we tried to explain it to the people we owed. But the company finally wrote letters of explanations to everyone and paid all fees that were charged to correct the situation. Sound ludicrous? And if they paid the fees, what was the problem, right?

The problem in dealing with faith is we can sometimes put our trust in the wrong thing. My husband had faith in the company he worked for. They were well established and growing rapidly. But sometimes we misdirect our faith. Don't get me wrong. My husband did then, and still does, have complete faith in God. That was just an illustration to show how we misdirect our faith at times. It's sorta like when we start our cars each morning. We believe it will start or we wouldn't wait until the last minute to run out the door to go to church. But how do we point our faith in the right direction?

God's Word declares, "…faith cometh by hearing and hearing by the Word." (Romans 10:17) The hard part comes when you try to reason this out by what you see. With true faith in God, one doesn't have to resort to Plan B.

Getting saved came at a time when I was just developing my reasoning skills, so walking by faith was new to me. Even God says, "Come now, let us reason together…" (Isaiah 1:18) So why was I having such a hard time?

For one thing, I'd been taught that a lot of it was emotional. You had to go to the altar and *pray though.* I believe in praying through because now I know there are principalities with which we struggle. But at the time I didn't. All I knew was some bad experiences at a local church.

I remember one in particular where I felt the tugging of the Holy Spirit although I didn't understand it then. I just knew that if I didn't do something, I would literally burst or choke to death on the knot in my throat. So I did what others were doing. I stepped out to go to the altar, not knowing what would happen when I got there.

As I approached the short-legged table and knelt, others began to surround me. In their zeal to see another lost sheep return to the fold, they scared the living heebie jeebies out of me. Questions filled my mind but previous experience had already taught me that your left arm did not question older people. They knew what was best for you.

Now you must understand. I had had no biblical training at all except for what I was able to pick up from other people's conversations. I had always been told to be good if I wanted to go to heaven. I didn't know what sin was. I didn't know about the cross. I didn't know much of anything except how to hide when the drunken cursing and fighting began at home. I was only ten years old so in my eyes, I was not lost. I knew exactly where I was. I knew the name of the church, the name of the town, the name of the one that brought me. So how was I lost? I even knew the way back home in case the one that brought me got tired of me asking questions? Scared? You bet!

But like an obedient child, I began to do what they said. They told me to confess that I was a sinner. I didn't know what that meant but it had to be good because all these people were helping me do it. Maybe this God that made them have so much energy and run a lot would hear me and if He thought I was a good enough sinner, He might like me, too. That's all I wanted anyway, was for someone to like me. OK. I'd be a sinner. So far the results looked pretty good.

Now came the painful and confusing part. The people that took me to church had said that some of the church members were double minded, unstable in all their ways. It didn't sound good when they said it and now these same people were down here telling me what to say to God.

I knew enough to know that the mind was in the head and in school we were taught there was one brain in the head. So if these people had two minds, it was no wonder they couldn't get it together. Needless to say, it came as no surprise when one would slap me on the left arm and yell, "Hang on, Sister!" And the other would slap me on the right arm and yell, "Let go, Sister!" They thought I was crying from joy at admitting I was a sinner when in reality I was in pain.

Actually, I didn't know what to hang onto or let go of unless it was my confession to being a sinner. And I certainly didn't want to let go of that because I had a feeling this was the only kind of people God dealt with. Finally the time came when one of the ladies smiled and said, "Do you feel like God saved you?"

Oh, yes, I thought. He did. You were beating me to a pulp and you stopped. So I would say He saved me from what I perceived to be almost the worst kind of torture. But I couldn't understand what I had done to these people to make them dislike me so much as to hit me. As for being a sinner…I reasoned that it had taken a few minutes for them to stop hitting me and being a sinner must mean something along the line of how long you would endure a beating. Sorta like being initiated into a club. I figured I'd done pretty well because I had lasted through the whole thing.

Maybe God thought I was tough because I didn't run away and by the way these ladies were now hugging me, I thought being double minded might not be so bad because He was just trying to get them to see if I measured up. But then again, it was quite painful and scary and the preacher had said God loved people.

Maybe I should just keep my eyes and ears open for a while and lay low. It left me quite uncertain about God.

Of course, in some ways it was like being right at home. I never knew what kind of mood my parents would be in either. Laying low wasn't all that hard. I had a great deal of practice in it so I figured after a while I could learn what this Guy was up to and what He expected from me. So watch Him I did, and a few days later it all came home to me.

I was assigned to cafeteria duty at school and when I got back to class, I had to write 100 times, "I must not talk in class." Now that didn't make sense to me because I hadn't even been there. I was tired, I was scared all the time and that made me mad.

This teacher had been very nice to me in a lot of ways, so I figured we were buddies. Buddies can be truthful with each other, right? So when I told her she wasn't being fair it didn't go over as well as I thought it would. I not only had to write 100 sentences about talking in class, but she gave me fifty more for talking back. Teachers were stricter then than they are now and students behaved better. It might not have always been fair, but we knew to obey.

On the way home that day, I told a girl I thought the teacher was a creep. She gasped and said, "I thought you got saved. Saved people don't talk about others like that! You better go get saved again."

Oh, boy. I had blown it. Now I had to go back and get another beating and after telling God I was already a sinner, I wasn't sure if He would believe me this time. Now I was scared. But wait!! This girl's mother was one of the double-minded people at the altar with me. Being double-minded might make you unstable but if a person had two minds then they surely must know more about God than I did. And being unstable in all her ways couldn't be that bad. So she washed dinner dishes one night and left them the next. What was so bad about that? I decided to go see her.

She told me the first time I got saved was by Grace. (How many times are people allowed to get saved, anyway?) I didn't know who Grace was but I figured she must be all right. She said since I had already backslid, (and I knew that wasn't true because I hadn't lost my balance or stumbled all day long) I needed to go get saved again. This time it had to be by Faith.

Now let me see. The first time I got saved was confessing to God I was a sinner. I supposed He had told this lady Grace and that's how she came to save me instead of Him. Was she one of the ladies at the altar with me? Now I was no longer as good a sinner as I wanted to believe, so I had to go get saved again. Maybe if I cried harder He would feel sorry for me and wouldn't let the ladies hit me so much. Boy, it would sure be a lot easier if God would make an appearance once in a while. After much deliberation and really thinking that through, I ask my girlfriend's mother, "But what if God is mad at me and wont' let me get saved again?"

"He has to. Faith is the key to getting through to God," she explained.

Thanking her and walking away, I vowed I would get to know Grace and Faith pretty well. So the next day at school I ask my teacher (I wasn't mad at her any more) if she knew a lady named Grace.

"Oh, yes," she replied. "Why do you ask?"

"I was just wondering if she knew God."

"Not this Grace," she chuckled.

"Do you know any others?"

"No, 'fraid not."

"Do you know one named Faith?"

"Yes, but she's dead now."

Through my childish eyes, that was the worst thing she could have said. That was supposed to be the one God would save me through again.

Faith soon went out the window when I realized I'd never meet her. By the time I was a teenager, I had learned faith wasn't a person, but I was too busy to develop my faith. At about the age of fourteen we had moved again and I had the usual task of finding someone to take me to church. It turned out that my Sunday school teacher taught extensively about the plan of salvation.

When he began to expound on every one being a sinner my antennas went up. Without letting any one know, I took in every word he said. I learned that being a sinner was nothing to be proud of, and the truth of the matter was, everyone was guilty. UH-Oh. Sin was very bad.

You must realize how I grew up. I was alone, scared, and my role models in the home just didn't take time to know I lived there, too. I thought it was natural to have a lot of drinking and fighting in the home. I thought all parents beat each other when they got mad and all kids spent most of their time hidden behind the dresser. To me these things weren't wrong but natural. I didn't like it but I knew better than to argue with my parents about it. And here this guy was telling me sin was a bad thing.

In a nutshell he said breaking our law was a crime…breaking God's was a sin. No one could keep all of God's laws. That's why we needed Grace. "And what was Grace?" he would ask, then smile and continue with a whisper, "Undeserved favor."

This man would tell us how mankind had rebelled against God and getting saved was reconciliation between man and God: a reconciliation brought about through the blood that His Son, Jesus had shed on Calvary. Faith, it turned out, was believing in something you could not see; complete blind trust. I could do that. After all, I couldn't see pain either, but I sure did believe in it.

He explained we must get forgiveness for our sins. Sin caused separation from God. This shocked me. I went to school, I came home, did my chores, helped cook dinner and I did my homework. On the weekends I helped give the whole house a thorough cleaning and I secretly admired a certain boy at school. Secretly, because in those days, at fourteen, good girls did not date, at least that's what I was taught. You had to be sixteen. So what had I done to earn this separation? *It's in my blood? How did it get there? Wow! I had inherited it? From whom? Adam?!!!*

You mean my great, great, great, (and on it goes) grandfather separated me from God at birth and I didn't even know it? And in doing that he abandoned me to the care of someone else? Why didn't somebody tell me I was a foster child? My biological forefather had really done a number on me. He had actually put me up for adoption. So who, pray tell, was my foster parent?

It reminded me of my own father. He cut out without bothering to see me grow up. Whoops! Wait a minute. If God was the beginning, and He created Adam, and Adam didn't do what he was supposed to do, then naturally he got into trouble. Undoubtedly his left arm didn't listen. Sounds to me like the State stepped in and took us because it didn't like the way we were being raised, as if they could do better. Yeah, right!

OK. Let's reason this out. God provided for us in every way. Just like our parents are supposed to do. Adam didn't listen. Just like my dad. From what he was saying, this guy thought God would never do anything for us to be taken away from Him so it wasn't neglect or abandonment. So what happened? Seems to me something is missing here.

My mother always told me not to get into cars with strangers. So I pictured it like this: The devil came along. He offered Adam a ride and even offered him candy so he would get into the car. Adam sure wanted that candy and maybe, Adam reasoned, God just didn't know this character very well. After all, God was up in heaven most of the time and this guy was here in the garden with him and Eve. By her not being afraid of him, he must be pretty nice. And oh, that candy sure did look good.

One bite. God will never know. One bite and WHAM! Adam was in the car. So God didn't place us in a foster home. WE WERE KIDNAPPED!

And by Adam and Eve both being kidnapped they were both in bondage. As they multiplied, their offspring were in bondage, too. The sad thing is with each passing generation the reality of being in bondage began to dim. Each generation thereafter began to think life was normal and all was well. Just like me. So what was the ransom? *Blood?*

It was beginning to make sense to me. This man who had entered my life and took the time to tell me of this, rather than make me go to the altar and get beaten to death, was also the youth leader of the church. Sunday after Sunday he would stand and tell us the story of how Jesus paid the ransom. But to me, it appeared that someone forgot to tell the kidnapper.

I didn't realize the kidnapper was completely aware of it and was constantly trying to keep us from knowing the truth. To me, a scared, lonely confused kid, this whole thing sounded a little farfetched. Sorta like when I learned there was no Santa Claus. Someone had lied to me again. Actually, I should have known there was no Santa Claus because I wasn't such a bad kid and he always left plenty of presents for the girl down the street and she was always in trouble. There was actually one Christmas we received a lot of big presents. A few weeks later a truck pulled up and started loading every thing. I learned Santa didn't pay his bills either. Maybe Santa stayed drunk and couldn't always find our house. To me, the whole thing was bogus.

I had just discovered everyone was a sinner. I didn't have the monopoly on the thing and to make matters worse, I had inherited this whole business. Now he was telling me I had to believe. In *what?*

I had been told if I were good, Santa would bring me something for Christmas. I was and he didn't. I had been told my dad loved me, but he cut out. I had been told my mother was the only one that really cared about me (this was from my mother, of course) but she didn't have time for me with the fights and the men when my dad was away. And this was love?

Now this guy wanted me to believe Someone loved me enough to die for me so I could be reconciled with God because my ancestors had messed up royally before I was born? And to beat it all, he said I had to believe in my heart. How does one believe in one's heart? Don't we think and reason with our head? I didn't know of all the scriptures that tell us about believing in our heart. I was not old enough or intelligent enough to reason this out, but I had been told so much that didn't make sense or eventually turned out to be a lie, I no longer trusted anyone. At the same time I didn't want anyone to know how confused I was, or how badly I was hurting inside.

I wasn't aware that the heart and not the brain or mind had any thing to do with it. Actually, I didn't know the mind was really the seat of the heart, at least the emotional one. Recently, I learned some great stuff on this. These are actually things I've learned through the years, but until now, have been hard to put into words.

Proverbs 23:7 tells us that as a man thinketh in his heart so is he. How many parents out there really take the time to listen to their children and learn how they think in their hearts? Children have a hard time. Things bother them. Young tikes as well as teens. And it is up to the parents to help them work through their problems and fears instead of making them feel their thoughts or feelings are stupid. And we also need to understand that sometimes a parent will expect too much from their child and the responsibility is overwhelming. The child can never meet the expectations and so they resort to finding approval elsewhere. Your child's heart is tender and impressionable.

A tremendous step toward living for God is for one to be able to have control over his or her thoughts. If you are not careful, the spirit of this age will control the majority of your thoughts and you will not be thinking about the wonderful things of God or His Word…like His plan for salvation.

Parents need to take time to fully explain salvation to their children. I'm not talking about what they hear others tell them. I'm talking about really sitting down with your children and showing them scripture. I stayed confused most of my first twenty-four years. And I was afraid to ask some of the adults to explain things to me.

I secretly wondered why confessing I was a sinner was supposed to be so great. I didn't even know what a sinner was as a child. I secretly wondered why I had to get saved over and over again. I didn't, but that's what I was taught. It seemed I could never please God because I certainly did not want to get another beating. And this incident really happened to me. My skinny arms were red as blisters when they got through with me. No one took time to tell me I didn't have to get saved over and over again.

I know now that this is not the way it really happened. I know now Adam and Eve chose to listen to Satan instead of obeying and all of mankind has inwardly been looking for spiritual peace since then. Most just look in the wrong direction. Peace, joy, and laughter were almost taboo at my house. It was an environment where fear and hate dominated. The misery that was welcomed into the house was so strong it literally sucked the life right out of you. But I was a kid and being kidnapped was the only way I could reason things out in my mind. I was a grown woman with two children before someone came into my life and taught me how to be a wife and mother according to the Word.

Parents, PLEASE, listen to your kids. Let them admit they wanted to cheat on that test. Don't punish them for admitting to something they didn't give in to. They fought the temptation. Shouldn't you rejoice? We always told our children if they got a "D" on their report cards and if we knew without a shadow of a doubt they did their best, then that "D" was acceptable and together we would work to improve it. But if we knew they had not spent enough time preparing or studying the way they should, then they knew they were in deep trouble.

Let your daughters admit they think the new boy in school is the greatest thing since baked cinnamon rolls (with raisins). Let them admit they have thoughts about love, childbirth, drugs and peer pressure. And most of all let them admit they might sometimes question the existence of God. You don't have to excuse it but let them share with you and talk to them without judgment. If you will admit it, you probably had the same thoughts when you were a kid.

After all the thoughts of the heart have been spoken, give them scripture that will show them their thoughts are normal and scripture that will help them make the best decisions. If you do not teach them how to make the right choices now with all the things that you may think are silly, then they will gradually withdraw from you and choose their own road and it may not be the healthiest choice.

Once when our son, Tony, was in about the eighth grade, I got a call from the principal one morning saying he was very ill and was throwing up. This alarmed me because he had been born with a blood disease that kept us on our toes. Saying I was on my way, I immediately left work and went to school.

After I had picked him up and we were seated in the car, I asked, "Son, are you all right?"

"Yes, ma'am," was his reply.

So trying to teach him sound judgment concerning his disease, I said, "Well, I see no evidence that your platelets are running wild, but do you think you need to see the doctor?"

"No, ma'am."

"What happened to make you so sick?"

"Do you promise not to get mad if I tell you?"

"What have we always told you, Tony?"

"That if I tell you the truth, it will not be as bad for me because you would rather hear the truth from me than someone else?"

"Exactly. Now what happened?"

"Some of the guys were pressuring me into trying a cigarette. I did. And it didn't set to well. I've been throwing up ever since I tried it."

Holding back a laugh because I wanted him to know the seriousness of his actions, I asked, "Do you think you will want to smoke again?"

"No, ma'am. I've experimented enough."

And it was settled. I did not make him feel condemned. I did not threaten to kill him when I got him home, nor did I threaten him with his dad. (Why do women do that anyway? Are they trying to make the dad look like the bad guy?) I didn't tell him how stupid he was. It was settled!! He's now thirty-four and guess what? He doesn't smoke. Plus!!! We've learned a lot since then and Tony has been healed.

But the whole episode of people misleading me, and the teacher trying so hard to get us to understand salvation had a lasting effect on me. This man was telling me something of importance but I'd been lied to so much I decided to shut it out. How could I believe or have faith in my heart when it was quite a few inches from my brain? But I began to read the Bible like he said and I began to know the Book pretty well. The trouble was it would be several years before I got to know the Author.

During this time it was merely printed words to me. You see, Jesus said in John 10 that His sheep know His voice. While tied up with the bonds of reasoning and in the custody of the devil, he didn't mind if I read the Book, as long as I didn't hear the voice of the Author. He knew the Truth was hidden from me by all the people and rotten deals in my life; all the ones that helped keep me bound, and most of them actually thought they were doing the right thing.

Keeping the truth hidden is not hard. And whether you like it or not, it's usually the church crowd that does it best. A good example of this would be something I saw and heard one Halloween night.

I had gone to the local grocery store and as I got out of the car, I heard strong aggressive shouting. I turned toward the commotion and there on the corner was a group of church people grabbing the arms of some of the young teens that were dressed in Halloween attire and yelling at them, "You're going to hell!"

These teens and the parents of the younger children were stopping in their tracks and wondering what they had done to bring such hostility their way. One small child was so scared his voice trembled as he cried, *"Daddy?"* His father simply laid his hand on his shoulder and ushered him around them only to be told, "You're sending your child to hell!" Finally the teens had had enough and began to get sarcastic and smart with the church people. I was so ashamed. I was ashamed for what my so-called brothers and sisters were doing to this group of ignorant people. And ignorant simply means without knowledge. I shuddered to think of what kind of impression this left on that small child and the anger that was probably aroused in the teens at being judged.

When you speak to people concerning their salvation let me suggest to you that you get your facts straight and watch your attitude. If you will look in the four gospels you will find the Messiah never spoke to the lost that way. And I hate to burst your bubble, but it was actually the church crowd He rebuked. The Pharisees, the Sadducees, and the ones that belonged to a denomination. And these people were really denominations and ours is quickly and just as stubbornly following in their footsteps.

When Jesus spoke to the lost He spoke with compassion and love. He spoke with compassion to Mary Magdalene, even the IRS in the form of Zacchaeus. And if you will look very closely, you will find He even spoke in a quiet manner to Judas Iscariot when He told him to take care of business, and that business was to betray Him. It had to be in a quiet manner because none of the men at the table understood what He was referring to. Look closely.

"Jesus answered, He it is to whom I shall give a sop, when I have dipped it. And when he had dipped the sop, he gave it to Judas Iscariot, the son of Simon.

And after the sop Satan entered into him. Then said Jesus unto him, Thou doest, do quickly.

Now no man at the table knew for what intent he spoke this unto him.

For some thought, because Judas had the bag that Jesus had said unto him Buy those things that we have need of against the feast; or that he should give something to the poor. (John 13:26-29 Italics added)

He knew Judas was going to betray Him and still He spoke softly, with love and compassion.

Most of the people in my life would give me just enough to make it sound good. Like a severely wounded person in the emergency room, I was given just enough care to relieve the pain but the Specialist was never called in. I never received the heart transplant I needed. These people were in as much bondage as I was and never knew it.

Spiritually my life was a mess. It had the resemblance of someone being in the emergency room after a terrible accident. I was conscious enough to know I needed help but not enough to know how to get it. I thought the 'pain medicine' I was receiving was a cure. I didn't know it only masked the symptoms. I didn't understand at the age of ten when I felt the tugging of the Holy Spirit and went to the altar that I did not have to hold on or let go. It wasn't necessary for the women to keep slapping me on the arms. All I had to do was yield. So figuratively, there I lay in the emergency room hooked up to the life supporting system of humanistic reasoning that served as a respirator, waiting for someone to cure me, or pull the plug and let me die.

Thankfully, someone came in that could deliver a cure, and it was in the form of the preacher…the one that actually led me to Christ in January 1975. In reality he told me of a Doctor that could help. And if I wanted to, he could call the Doctor for me. He had to; because I was so wounded I couldn't even speak. But a beautiful thing happened.

As he began to speak aloud to this Doctor (this was in the form of him leading me in the sinner's prayer) the respirator stopped working. Gasping for breath, I soon realized that I could breathe and with each breath, I called this Doctor's name, too. It was like I died and came back to life. As I gasped for breath, I did die. But it was so sudden, the only thing I felt was a lifting of a weight from my shoulders. I realized my death, at that moment, was actually dying to this world. Then just as suddenly, I started breathing again. And just as quickly the Doctor appeared. Although I had never seen Him, I knew Him. And He had come to remove my bonds and take me away from the kidnapper.

Something odd was happening. This Doctor must have come directly from surgery. He still had blood on His hands. No. The blood was seeping from wounds in His palms. I watched and as the blood dropped on my bonds…bonds of loneliness, rejection, and no longer able to trust…they began to burn away as if acid had just touched them.

Soon I was free and as I laid there in relief, He began to touch my chest. As He did this, the pain subsided. The aching was gone and He spoke ever so gently. "Hi," He smiled and whispered. "I've come to take you to your real family. You're no longer held hostage."

Now the reality of this amazing grace that led to my salvation took a while to sink in. Like I said, when I accepted Christ, the Messiah, as my personal Lord and Savior, there were no fireworks and the scene I just described was one that took place spiritually over a period of a few days. Remember, I had to walk on the naked truth.

Since then, I guess people think I've been in a coma, or hallucinating, because I can see things a lot of people can't see. I can see our church growing beyond belief with ministries branching out to the uttermost parts of the world. I can see families being reunited even though they are still miles apart.

You see, along with the heart transplant came faith and with the faith, although it was just a little at a time, my vision began to clear. And as my vision cleared I realized that my Redeemer had spoken to me at the age of ten, and I recognized His voice, but no one took the time to explain to me that I needed to answer and then just listen, because faith comes by hearing and hearing by the Word. It's really so simple.

It took me a while to realize that being a part of His household meant certain things, like He was the Head. In the structure of the family, God says the man is the head and in some countries, no matter how old a man gets, if his father is still alive, then his father is still the head. The father says what is to happen within the family. He directs everyone whether they agree or not.

By the time I'd been saved several years, I had learned that listening and obedience were vital, but was having a hard time getting new converts, and even older ones in my class to grasp the depth of this. It was easy for them to have faith as long as they could see things going the right way. But once an obstacle appeared, their faith dwindled. My husband and I have a joke between us for these kinds of people. If things spoken in faith do not materialize within twenty-four hours then we wait to see if they resort to Plan B. Of course, Plan B is just what the devil wants. So nothing would go right and the next thing you know, he's handing out candy again.

One day Colossians 1:18 caught my attention. I thought since people in other countries put so much store in the wisdom of the aged, and the father is always the head, then the wisdom of my heavenly Father had to be gigantic. And since the fullness of the Godhead is in Christ, then He should know it all. No wonder He is the Head of the Body.

My head had gotten me in trouble more than once but I was still curious as to how His Head related to *my* body. Better yet, how did my head relate to His? Why did we need His Head instead of our own? After a while, I found out.

I was given a copy of a prayer that was supposed to have been spoken at the opening of a new session of the Kansas Senate. When Minister Joe Wright began to speak, everyone was expecting the usual generalities, but this is what they heard:

"Heavenly Father, we come before you today to ask Your forgiveness and to seek Your direction and guidance. We know Your Word says, "Woe to those who call evil good" but that is exactly what we have done. We have lost our spiritual equilibrium and reversed our values. We confess that. We have ridiculed the absolute truth of Your Word calling it Pluralism. We have endorsed perversion and called it alternative lifestyle. We have exploited the poor and called it the lottery. We have rewarded laziness and called it welfare. We have killed our unborn and called it choice. We have shot abortionists and called it justifiable. We have abused power and called it politics. We have coveted our neighbor's possession and called it ambition. We have polluted the

air with profanity and pornography and called it freedom of expression. We have rid-iculed the time-honored values of our forefathers and called it enlightenment.

Search us, oh, God, and know our hearts today. Cleanse us from every sin and set us free. Guide and bless these men and women who have been sent to direct us to the center of Your will. We ask it in the name of Your Son, the living Savior, Jesus Christ.

Amen

3

Christ the Head

During my years of serving the Lord, I've heard very few sermons on the Head; sermons on the Rock, the Great Physician, the Deliverer, the Soon Coming King, yes, but very few on the Head. There have been a lot on my husband being the head of the house, but the teachings on Christ being the Head usually turned out to be just a quote from the Bible.

Paul had a great teaching in I Corinthians 11:1-16. I think this passage has been abundantly misused to show that Paul taught the woman was inferior to the man when in reality I don't think his superiority or her inferiority had any thing to do with it. So for now, we'll simply look at the passage and tie it in with Christ being the Head and not my inferiority to my husband. The passage reads:

"Be ye followers of me, even as I also am of Christ. Now I praise you, brethren, that ye remember me in all things, and keep the ordinances as I delivered them to you. But I would have you know, that the head of every man is Christ: and the head of woman is the man: and the head of Christ is God. Every man praying or prophesying, having his head covered, dishonoreth his head. But every woman that prayeth or prophesieth with her head uncovered dishonoreth her head: for that is even all one as if she were shaven. For if the woman be not covered, let her also be shorn: but if it be a shame for a woman to be shorn or shaven, let her be covered. For a man indeed ought not to cover his head, for as much as he is the image and glory of God: but the woman is the glory of the man. For this cause ought the woman to have power on her head because of the angels. Nevertheless neither is the man without the woman, neither the woman without the man, in the Lord. For as woman is of the man, even so is the man also by the woman; but all things of God. Judge in yourselves; is it comely that a woman pray unto God uncovered: Doth not even nature itself teach you, that, if a man have long hair, it is a shame unto him? But if a woman have long hair, it is a glory to her; for her hair is given her for a covering. But if a man seem to be contentious, we have no such custom, neither the churches of God."

This is the order of things: God, Christ, man, woman. This in no way implies woman is inferior to man. There is another purpose for this illustration. Let's examine it.

The main frame of the passage is the covering of the head. Is it permissible or not? Some denominations look at this to prove or disprove if a person, be it man or woman, should cut their hair. In one denomination a few years ago, the women could not cut their hair, but they insisted a man cut his. Of course, it's different now. Somewhere along the line, they decided it wasn't a sin any more. But the length of the hair is not the issue here. The point is the covering and the God-ordained order of things and how it should be used during prayer or prophesying. The *type* of covering is also taught.

Look at verse four. According to this, if a man prays or prophesies with his head covered, it dishonors his head. What is his head? Christ. So if he covers it, he is dishonoring Christ. He's cutting the line of communication and in our line of thinking, it would appear man is putting a barrier between him and Christ. Let me back up and give you a little background so you can fully grasp what I'm about to say.

There is a website you can visit that shows the Western Wall, (some call it the Wailing Wall) in Jerusalem. You can type a prayer request and someone in Jerusalem will get it and put it in one of the holes in the wall. Some verses in the Bible have, on occasion, had me completely stumped, and I was tired of getting different interpretations from people of the cloth. Usually based on their denomination, it will be interpreted according to their basic beliefs. A lot of times if you're not careful, the power of suggestion can automatically make you see things in the scriptures that really aren't there. So I typed a prayer that simply said, "Lord, teach me Your Torah." Within two weeks I had met several Messianic rabbis and they referred me to the writings and interpretations of other Messianic rabbis. These rabbis were very well trained in the Jewish language so with that, I had no problem studying the teachings. I really feel if any should know the correct interpretations, it will be someone that knows the language. Some of these teachings made my goose bumps have goose bumps. The teachings have changed my way of looking at things and the Word. So much so, that now the Torah is not a list of ordinances to beat us over the head, but a way of life.

I was always taught the verse in Genesis 3:16 where God told Eve that her desire shall be to her husband was a sexual thing. But that's not true. The original literally means her desire to control. When God created everything He gave mankind, not man, but mankind, authority over the earth. We have dominion here. This is our domain. We rule! But when Adam sinned he forfeited that authority and gave it to Satan. God won't step in and take control unless we ask Him to because He cannot go against His own Word and He gave this world to us. That is why Jesus prayed, "Thy will be done on earth as it is in Heaven." He created man first, then woman and that is the order of things. So going back to the passage in I Corinthians concerning the hair, let's look at it from the angle of cutting the hair as interpreted by a Messianic Jew. Then we'll look at the real issue he is trying to convey to us and see that the Body has latched onto a hobbyhorse and won't let go.

Synagogue Customs

"Sometimes it is hard to relate to ancient biblical laws, teachings and customs, due to the modern day religious customs we have assumed. The fact is that many of our present day doctrines and dogmas have evolved by interpretations and insertions of our forefathers. Though they were very sincere, it is possible that some truths and facts could have been overlooked or unknown.

Have you ever visited a sanctuary, holy site, or went to join in prayer with some and find you were held at a distance, because of a difference in views or customs?

Let us trace some of our customs back to the first century C.E. (common or Christian Era). First it must be understood that all of Christianity had its roots in Judaism and that the only written laws and guidelines considered scripture was the Tenakh (Old Testament). For centuries the children of Israel had been taught how to approach unto, and present themselves before their God. This did not change with the appearance of the sect of the Nazarenes, as some might have you think. Yeshua (Jesus) himself was circumcised on the eighth day after his birth (Luke 2:21), and kept the Passover at Jerusalem (Luke 4:14-21). The Sabbath synagogue service has remained virtually unchanged since shortly after the Babylonian captivity. It replaced the Temple as the place of worship and was established for prayer, reading and studying the Law of Moses.

The great historian J. Robert Teringo wrote: "The fixed order of service began after the customary greeting, with a prayer while the people remained standing facing the sacred Torah scroll. The reading of the Law of Moses was next. The Torah scroll was taken from the chest and placed before a reader who read in the ancient Hebrew tongue and immediately translated it into Aramaic, the language of those days. A commentary was always added to this reading. Next, a portion was read from the books of the prophets and again, immediately translated verse by verse. After closing prayer, the service was concluded."

This order of service not only prevailed throughout the land of Palestine during the first century, but still continues around the world until the present time. The custom of attending synagogue was also deeply ingrained into the life of Saul of Tarsus (Paul the Apostle).

Also, it would be good at this time to mention that the dress and attire of the Jews differed much from the Greeks and Romans in many ways. The Jewish men took care to wear a head covering but the Greeks went bareheaded. The Greek and Roman carvings, statues, and paintings bear this out. Again referring to J. Robert Teringo:

"Covering for the head was important to all men: their hair and beards also received a great deal of attention and care. Most men kept their hair trimmed and clean and those who could afford it perfumed or anointed their hair for festive occasions. Boys and young men wore their hair short and thick, as a full head of hair was much esteemed."

The present day Orthodox Jewish sages would not uncover their heads because they believed God's glory was around them and over them. This could be based on the morning prayer, "Blessed by thou, O Lord, who crowns Israel with beauty."

In ancient Jewish beliefs there is found stern disapproval of the uncovered head, whether it be a man or a woman. When his head is unavoidable bared, he is forbidden to pronounce the name of God, to recite the Shema, or to read from the Torah. It is always recalled in this connection that, when the high priest entered the Holy of Holies in the Temple in Jerusalem on Yom Kippur, he first had to cover his head with his golden miter. Christians have often wondered why Jews put their hats on as a sign of reverence while they themselves take their hats off to express the same feeling. Yeshua and the early Jewish Christians, who adhered to this as well as many other Jewish customs, unquestionably covered their heads when they entered a synagogue or when they engaged in prayer.

The footnotes in the Zodhiates Hebrew Greek Study Bible referring to this subject of head coverings are as follows:

Paul is writing to the Corinthian Christians who, living in Greece, customarily complied with Greek traditions: men had their heads uncovered and the women covered theirs: which however, was contrary to the Jewish tradition. (Personal note of this author—this was a tradition only, not the law.)

The question, which faced the Corinthians, was what to do with the existing custom of their day. Paul's advice is to examine the symbolism of the custom. If it has nothing in it that is contrary to God's Word or order in creation, accept it. (Keep in mind here that when Paul told them to examine and compare it to God's Word, he was again referring to the Old Testament because there wasn't a New Testament at that time.) *Do not allow contentions to arise regarding customs, which symbolize something that is proper. In this case, the Greeks believed that by not covering their heads, the men declared the independence as contrasted to the slave who had to cover themselves. The women covered themselves, symbolizing the protectiveness that they enjoyed from their husbands. Paul intimated that there in nothing wrong with this, for in creation God created man, and from man there came the woman.*

Since this custom of head coverings showed beautifully that which is true in creation and also in the order of things, why should the Corinthian Christians living in Greece reject the Greek custom and assume the Jewish one? This decision, however, was left entirely to the Corinthians as we see in verse 13, which would have been far better translated "Decide in regard to it your own selves." Therefore, these are personal decisions which must be exercised in following a custom as long as the symbol is good and there is no contrary teaching involved in the symbolism. This whole Scripture teaches that existing customs, as long as they are not contrary to morals and Scripture, are to be adhered to for the sake of unity and not to be flaunted." In view of these findings as well as other historical facts, we must conclude that Apostle Paul, who himself was taught in the tradition and commandments of the Law, was not trying to establish another by forbidding men to wear a covering (hat or otherwise) before God in worship.

Therefore, the Sabbath service with reading from the Law and Prophets, the custom of the head covering, kippah for men and scarf for women, used by the Jews of Judea from before the first century even until now, seems to be biblical. But, like Apostle Paul said, if any man be contentious (over hair or head coverings), we have no such customs neither the congregations of God.

We can easily see here that Paul is trying to help the people in Corinth to understand the customs of the Jews handed down through the centuries, key word here being customs. And we have taken the whole content to make it a dogmatic teaching to show a woman should not cut her hair and a man would be better off bald. I say this harshly because a few years ago, our oldest son had been working extremely long hours, and had not had time to get a haircut. Normally, he tried to keep it military short but at that time, it was just touching his shirt collar really well.

One night he had gone to mid-week prayer service straight from work and before the service started the pastor walked up behind him, and grabbing his hair, jerked his head back and said, "Don't you think it's time you got that mop cut?"

This in itself was totally embarrassing but it was the final straw to a string of legalistic doctrines that he was questioning, so he did what any eighteen year old would do. He walked out. And do you have any clue how long it took us to get him to see it was the preacher that was condemning him, not Christ?

He now accepts the fact that Christ loves him because of his heart and not his hair but he decided then and there to wear it long, and looooong it is. He keeps it styled and very neat, but it is long. And I will be the first to admit, it looks good, very good. The problem with the whole thing was, what would have happened to him if he had not had parents that knew the Book and the Author so he could be guided? What if this had been a newly saved person that didn't know his position in the Body yet? Because of attitudes like that, he could have fallen by the wayside and never gotten up.

(Update!! Newsflash!!!) Since the finished writing of this book, and just in time for me to go back and insert the update before it went to the publisher, Tony got his hair cut. Back to military style, no less. All those years and he waits till now!!)

Back to the Scriptures. The order of things here is the issue. Paul said in verse four if a man prays or prophesies with his head covered, he dishonors his head. And in the next verse he says if a woman leaves her head uncovered she dishonors *her* head. Why? Because he says in verse seven a man is the image and glory of God but the woman is the glory of the man. (Did you hear that, Gene, I'm your glory, sweetheart?) Let's quickly put something to rest here. If a woman is the man's glory, how does that make her inferior? Pet peeve again…moving on.

So, if a woman uncovers (or pulls all her hair out) her literal head, she is showing her own egotistical glory and not the glory she is supposed to be showing, which is her husband's. With this verse alone we can easily say, "Strut your stuff, ladies, cause you make him shine."

However, if a man covers his literal head, he is preventing the glory of God from shining, which is the man. That ought to make a person feel really humble to know that we are the glory of God. But this simple fact is ignored and the Body chooses to argue and bicker over the length of someone's hair and how important a man or woman is, all the while forgetting that Christ is the Head, not us or our own convictions.

In my search for the exact meaning behind all of this, I began to notice most people take their bodies for granted and have never spent much time actually learning how the head governs the body nor never took the time to look at everything in two ways.

The precious words in the Bible are given to instruct us and when reading it, it is helpful to look at the physical and the spiritual realm. Actually, everything that happens to us should be looked at that way.

When a child plays with matches and gets burned, he soon learns to not play with matches. When trials come we should always ask ourselves, "What am I supposed to learn from this?" We are all members of the Body of Christ. Now try to picture this.

Take the portraits of Christ's face (that derived from man's imagination) and put the face or head on top of a body. Picture you own body, complete with a head and face, in some strategic area such as an index finger. I know someone who has a deliverance ministry for substance abuse. I once pictured her as part of the digestive tract, the lower part of the digestive tract. You know...the intestines.

Now why would I picture her, a very beautiful person, as a large intestine? Well, the intestines are used to rid the body of unwanted or unnecessary stuff. In the next few chapters we will take a look at the human body and tie it in with the scriptures. Each part in the head represents certain aspects of God, Jesus, the Holy Ghost and our every day way of living.

When doing this study, I soon realized how badly mislead or lacking our local churches of today are, and how we operate more on mere tradition than actually by the Word. It soon became obvious that many of our practices are man made and more and more we want the Word to line up with our life instead of our life lining up with the Word. The local church has let the world slip in so much that we have very little left to offer. We are so dogmatic on certain rituals that we no longer leave our mind open to what the Spirit is telling us. If it goes against the grain, we don't want to practice it.

Not only are we living according to man made traditions, but we are very quickly becoming immune to sin. We have accepted the rule of 'it's the lesser of the two evils', when we really don't have to accept any evil at all.

With all the talk of the new age movement, the dummy card, (whoops! I need to be politically correct...that's smart card) and big brother, I find it quite humorous that the governing bodies of the world think they can actually develop a computer system so complex it would control every aspect of our lives. Of course, according to the Bible, this will be true for a while. In Revelations 13:16, 17 we read, *"And he causeth all, both small and great, rich and poor, free and bond, to receive a mark in their right hand, or in their foreheads: And that no man might buy or sell, save he that had the mark, or the name of the beast, or the number of his name."*

The key to the failure of this magnificent system is to know Jesus as Lord because God will always have a remnant, someone who will make it through. Boy!! Talk about a computer glitch! So read my lips, big brother. You may have all the sophisticated equipment in the world, but we have One in Heaven, and we will win.

When we stop and think of the more complex system of the brain, with Christ being the head, then it only proves what the Bible says even more. *"But if any man be ignorant, let him be ignorant."* (I Corinthians 14:38) Does anyone out there think this verse applies to most of our world leaders as I do?

Go ahead. Build all the complex systems you want, Satan. And when you start having your programmer put in the appropriate dates, remember, you only have seven years then Christ will pull the plug. Just keep reading if you want to know more of the greatest complex system anywhere and its headquarters (get it? HEADquarters) is not Fort Meade, Maryland or Brussels, Belgium…it's Heaven.

4

The Conception

The entire nervous system is very complex. It has two parts: a central system and a peripheral system. The brain and spinal cord make up the central system (Christ the Head) and the vast network of nerves through out the rest of the body is the peripheral system (the congregation or Body of Christ). The peripheral nerves connect with the spinal cord so that information flows from these nerves to the brain and back again.

This basic information is vital in understanding the Body of Christ. For the expectant mothers, you should be aware that an embryo develops extremely rapidly. At five weeks it is about the size of a grain of rice and the nervous system is very obvious by six weeks. Although the embryo is less than an inch long, a basic primitive structure has developed. The central nervous system has already developed enough to be identified. Let me repeat. That's the *central nervous system.* But let's go back for a few weeks.

Conception is the fertilization of an egg by a sperm. For the first two weeks of cell division there is little differentiation between the kinds of cells produced. After this remarkable short period of two weeks, however, the embryo begins to develop different kinds of cells and primitive structures.

It is my desire, over the next few pages, to present to you a different concept of the Body of Christ. I've always been taught, and accepted, that the Church was born after Jesus arose from the dead and ascended into Heaven, that the Body of Christ came into being at this time. I still don't dispute parts of that; I just look at it a little more closely. Follow me on this and maybe you will agree. Now don't forget. We are not speaking of the *physical* body of our Lord, but the spiritual one, the Church, and its conception, gestation and birth.

Let's take a hypothetical situation here. Let's say we have a God ordained chain of events with this situation, instead of the loose morals of today and everything comes to pass in the order it is suppose to happen.

First we have a man that is single but has a deep-rooted desire to marry and have a family…in that order. His first step is to seek a bride and become engaged. He has never had relations with a woman, and he wants his bride to be the same way. He knows that in his loins is the seed that will give him the family he wants. His child is already there, waiting to do what is necessary to develop.

Now lets say this man finds the woman of his dreams, becomes engaged and later marries her. The union of man and woman takes place and eventually conception becomes a reality.

During the gestation, or development of the child there are some problems but nothing that cannot be overcome and dealt with, a few times of fear and doubt that the child would be born, but still the problems are rectified. Finally, the day arrives when the child moves into the birth canal, labor begins, and a delivery is made. That's physical. Now let's look at the spiritual.

The man desiring a wife and family is God. The seed to begin His family is already there in His loins. We see this in Proverbs 8:2-30 where it reads, *"the Lord possessed me in the beginning of His way, before His works of old. I was set up from everlasting, from the beginning, or ever the earth was. When there were no depths, I was brought forth, when there were no fountains abounding with water. Before the mountains were settled, before the hills was I brought forth. While as yet he had not made the earth, nor the fields, nor the highest part of the dust of the world. When He prepared the heavens, I was there; when he set a compass upon the face of the depth; when he established the clouds above; when he strengthened the fountains of the earth; Then I was by him, as one brought up with; and I was daily his delight, rejoicing always before him:"* (Italics added)

Before the beginning He was there, like the seed of man waiting for the seed of woman. In this modern day of technology, we can plan the size of our family. Inside every man there is a little Junior or Sally just waiting to be united with the seed of woman so he or she can start to grow into a body. *In the beginning,* He was there. Genesis 1:26 tells us, *And God said, let US make man in OUR image."* (Italics and capitalization added)

His next step was to find a bride and become engaged. In Gen. 12:1-3 we see the man, or God asking Israel to marry him. *"Now the Lord had said unto Abram, Get thee out of thy country, and from thy father's house unto a land that I will show thee: And I will make thee a great nation, and I will bless thee, and make thy name great; and thou shalt be a blessing: And I will bless them that bless thee, and curse him that curseth thee, and in thee shall all families of the earth be blessed."* (Italics added)

After an engagement the wedding takes place and she (Israel) becomes the wife and the union of God and Israel is consummated. Look at Genesis 17:10-16. This is beautiful.

In this passage God is telling Abraham that He wants to enter into a covenant with him, a blood covenant. This is done through circumcision. When a man and woman marry, if she is a virgin as God intended it to be in the natural order of things, when their union is complete, she will shed a little blood. In order for God's union to be complete with Israel, there had to be a little shedding of blood. But with the union came conception.

Remember we said at the first of the chapter that during the first two weeks of conception there is not much happening but a little cell division and even then there's not much difference in the cells. In Genesis 21:1-2 we see the first two weeks of gestation. *"And the Lord visited Sarah as he had said, and the Lord did unto Sarah as he had spoken. For Sarah conceived, and bare Abraham a son in his old age..."* (Italics added)

Now please understand, this verse, spiritually, is not showing the birth of Isaac, but cell division of the conceived church during the first two weeks of conception. We can see where the cells start to differentiate in Exodus 12:38. The Children of Israel were starting to leave Egypt. Everyone thinks of these people as all Jewish. Not so. This verse plainly tells us the cells had started to divide and be different. It reads, "And a *mixed* multitude went up also with them..." (Italics added)

The cells start to take on a variation and primitive structures begin to develop. The central nervous system is very obvious at this point. In our hypothetical situation we also said there would be some problems with the pregnancy, but nothing that could not be rectified. So here we have the desire, the engagement, the union, the conception, the first two weeks of gestation, the first six weeks showing primitive structures with the first one being a very pronounced central nervous system. Now the problems of a risky pregnancy have erupted. God also foretold of a difficult pregnancy for the Body of Christ.

Genesis 3:14-15 explains it. *And the Lord God said unto the serpent, Because thou has done this, thou are cursed above all cattle, and above every beast of the field; upon thy belly shalt thou go, and dust shalt thou eat all the days of thy life; and I will put enmity between thee and the woman, and between thy seed and her seed; it shall bruise thy head, and thou shall bruise his heel."* (Italics added)

All through history, in the Bible, we find where Satan tried to abort the pregnancy. He did everything he could to stop it. He knew there would be a birth, he just didn't know when. In Exodus he tried destroying all the babies, (Exodus

1:16) but Moses' mother hid him in the bulrushes of Egypt. Still Satan didn't give up. Man! You can give that liar an inch and he will try to be a ruler.

He called Planned Parenthood and made an appointment for counseling concerning whether this pregnancy should continue or not. (Matthew 1:19) But God had a Spirit filled counselor working there (Matthew 1:20) so the pregnancy would continue. Now remember, we are still talking about the church, the Body of Christ, not the physical body of our Lord as a babe.

Like I said before, I always thought the Body or Church came into being after Calvary. But most people forget that for a child or body to be born, there must be a time of development inside the womb. This is still the embryo of the church; it just hasn't made its appearance yet. And for those that don't see it this way, let me ask you something. If the Body of the Church didn't actually begin earlier with a developing period, why do we fight abortion so hard? Do we not believe the baby is already a living, breathing being before it is born? Likewise the Church. We are the Body of Christ and as a Body we had to have a developing period before a growth into adulthood period.

When Christ was born and Herod tried to find Him that he might slay Him, God warned Joseph, telling him to take the Child and His mother and flee into Egypt. (Matthew 2:13) This is the same place where His children were held captive.

When a baby is in the confines of the mother's womb, there isn't much room. Every mother knows what it's like to have a baby stretch and feel like it's cutting off her oxygen supply. The baby wants ROOM!! He doesn't understand that the place he is being held captive is also his hiding place, a place to find nourishment and develop. Not only is the time spent in Egypt a scary time for the pregnancy but, later, during the fetal stage, it borders on horror. There are times when the Body was in far greater danger of being a miscarriage like the captivities from Assyria and Babylon. We read the account of this in II Kings 17 and II Kings 24:17-20.

OK. So the pregnancy is difficult. You have some pea brain on the side trying to abort, and the Body of Christ is seeking more room to develop. In order to develop properly to full capacity (a perfectly formed fetus) it needs room.

Finally, it enters the birth canal and guess what! The Head comes first. Yes, sir, the CENTRAL NERVOUS SYSTEM has made its entrance. Jesus is that central nervous system because He is the Head. Israel was the wife. The child is all the people that were looking for a Redeemer and a Messiah in faith, and all the Christians, or reproduced cells thereafter to show how the Church must grow into adulthood. And the gates of hell shall not prevail against it, even after it reaches adulthood.

But even the central nervous system cannot function unless there is life in the blood. In Matthew 3:16, we see where the Body took its first breath of air and then it began to grow. *"and Jesus, when he was baptized, went up straightway out of the water; and lo, the heavens were opened unto him, and he saw the Spirit of God descending like a dove, and lighting upon him"* (Italics added)

Watch this carefully, none of my reference material showed which came first, the actual first breath of the baby or the severing of the umbilical cord (that which sustains life for the child until it becomes a separate entity). After making several calls I found one person that would answer my questions without thinking I was a medical student that was just too lazy to go to the library and look it up.

Anyway, she said usually the baby breathes before the cord is cut unless the infant is having trouble getting its first breath, and then it is quickly cut and respiratory measure are taken.

Remember we said in Matthew 3:16 we read that the baby, or the Body of Christ, the Church, took its first breath? The same Greek word is used in John 20:22. Jesus breathed on the disciples and said, "Receive ye the Holy Ghost," which would give the words Spirit and Ghost the same meaning.

In Genesis 1:2 we read where the Spirit of God moved upon the face of the waters. The word 'rauch' is used here and it means Spirit or wind. When checking in two dictionaries I saw the word 'wind' meant 'breath'. In other words, Genesis 1:2 could read, *"the breath of God moved upon the face of the waters."* (Italics added) Examine closely the next few sentences and meaning of words because it will help you get into the *Spirit* of things.

◆　　◆　　◆

Genesis 2:7 says that God breathed into his (man's) nostrils the breath of life; and man became a living soul. The word for soul is 'nephesh' and it means to be animated or brought to life. In Matthew 10:28 Jesus told His disciples not to fear the one that could destroy the body, but the One that could destroy both body and soul in hell. The word used for soul in Matthew 19:28 is 'psucho' and it means the same thing, to be animated or brought to life.

God told Moses the children of Israel could not eat the blood with the flesh *"for the life of all flesh is in the blood."* (Leviticus 17:14 Italics added) The Hebrew word for life in this passage is 'nephesh' which is the same word used in Genesis 2:7 and Matthew 10:28 for soul but in the passage it means—you got it—breath.

Last, but not least, in John 5:21, Jesus says the Father raises the dead and quickens them. The word 'quicken' comes from the Greek word 'zoopoieo' and it means to preserve life. However, in John 6:63 he says it is the Spirit that quickens. Is this a contradiction? No.

We are instructed to rightly divide the Word of Truth in II Timothy 2:15. We have already seen that the Spirit is none other than the breath of God. (That should make a Christian shiver to know that God's breath is actually flowing through us.) If it is the Father that quickens as in John 5:21, then it stands to reason that He will use a product, His breath (His Spirit) to do the quickening or preserving of life.

One good example would be the museum might exhibit a display of bottled life forms preserved in a liquid. The display card may read, "Insects preserved by Dr. So and So." Now is it Dr. So and So that did the preserving or the liquid (formaldehyde) that did it? Likewise, the Father is Dr. So and So and the liquid is the sweet Holy Ghost, or His breath.

So now the Head of the Body is here and has partaken of the breath of life. However, the umbilical cord still needs to be severed. The life sustaining force that connects the baby to the mother who is one with her husband. The cord was cut at Calvary when Jesus cried, *"Eloi, Eloi, lama sabachthani?" which being interpreted, my God, my God, why hast Thou forsaken me?"* (Mark 15:34 Italics added)

Oh, but the glory of it all is that He had already breathed the breath of life and on the third day He arose!!. He arose and His Body, the Church, began to grow into adulthood.

5

The Protection

Psalms 91

He that dwelleth in the secret place of the most High shall abide under the shadow of the Almighty. I will say of the Lord, He is my refuge and my fortress: my God: in him will I trust. Surely he shall deliver thee from the snare of the fowler, and from the noisome pestilence. He shall cover thee with his feathers, and under his wings shalt thou trust; his truth shall be thy shield and buckler. Thou shalt not be afraid for the terror by night; nor for the arrow that flieth by day. Nor for the pestilence that walketh in darkness; nor for the destruction that wasteth at noonday. A thousand shall fall at thy side, and ten thousand at thy right hand; but is shall not come nigh thee. Only with thine eyes shalt thou behold and see the reward of the wicked. Because thou hast made the Lord, which is my refuge, even the most High, thy habitation. There shall no evil befall thee, neither shall any plague come nigh thy dwelling. For he shall give his angels charge over thee, to keep thee in all thy ways. They shall bear thee up in their hands, lest thou dash thy foot against a stone. Thou shalt tread upon the lion and adder; the young lion and the dragon shalt thou trample under feet. Because he hath set his love upon me, therefore will I deliver him. I will set him on high, because he hath known my name. He shall call upon me, and I will answer him: I will be with him in trouble: I will deliver him, and honor him. With long life will I satisfy him, and show him my salvation.

As mentioned earlier, the central nervous system is in two parts: the brain and the spinal cord. The brain lies well protected within the rigid bony case of the skull. Bone has, as one of its components, calcium, which is also found in rock.

In Matthew 16:18 Jesus told His disciples *"...upon this rock I will build my church."* In this verse the Greek word for rock is 'petra', meaning a large stone. In Daniel 2:34 we find where a stone is cut out without hands and smites the image upon its feet, thus breaking it to pieces. The word for stone is 'eben' (Chaldean, meaning to build. In Ephesians 2:20 we see the Christ as the cornerstone. So it seems very appropriate that a skull would encase the brain because Jesus, in speaking of the Church, said in Matthew 16:18, *"the gates of hell shall not prevail against it."* (Italics added)

◆   ◆   ◆

The brain consists of three main parts: the paired cerebral hemisphere, the cerebellum, and the brain stem. Colossians 2:9 says, "for in Him dwelleth all the fullness of the Godhead BODILY". (Capitalization added) I believe these three parts represent the Father, the Son, and the Holy Ghost.

In John 14:9 Jesus says, "if you have seen me you have seen the Father." Also in John 10:30 He says, "I and my Father are one." So far we have two main parts, the paired cerebral hemispheres and the cerebellum or the Father and the Son. Remember, one brain, (I and My Father are one) representing three Persons—all the fullness of the Godhead bodily. Now for the third part, the brain stem, or the Holy Ghost.

In John 4:24 we read that God is a Spirit. Later in John 15:26 Jesus tells His disciples, "when the Comforter has come, whom I will send unto you from the Father, even the Spirit of truth, which *proceedeth* from the Father, He shall testify of Me." (Italics added)

The word 'proceedeth' in Greek is 'ekporeuomai' and it literally means to go out of. When a mother delivers a baby the child is going out of her. To emphasize the point here, think back to Genesis 2:24 where we are told that a man shall cleave unto his wife and they shall be one flesh. They are one, even though they are two.

Jesus said He and the Father are one. When a baby is being developed or born, that baby is a separate entity but is joined by the umbilical cord to its mother, making one. We've established that a man and a woman, even though they are two people, become one. So if a woman becomes one with her husband, and the baby is one with the mother, we have three in one, or the trinity, or a good picture of the brain representing the Father, the Son, and the Holy Ghost.

Earlier we said the paired cerebral hemispheres represent something within themselves. In John 10:30 Jesus said, "I and My Father are One." These two hemispheres are connected by the corpus callosum, which, according to my buddy Webster, is the great bank of commissural fibers (a connecting band of nerve tissue in the brain or spinal cord) uniting the cerebral hemispheres in man and higher mammals.

I like to think the band of nerves connecting these two hemispheres represents the Holy Ghost and the two parts as the Father and Son. The reason for this is,

Jesus has already said that He and the Father are one. That accounts for the two hemispheres. We know that nerves are used to transmit and receive messages from the brain and since the corpus callosum is a band of nerve tissues we can plainly see the connection and the resemblance of the Holy Ghost, because of what is recorded in Romans 8:26-27. It reads, "likewise the Spirit helpeth our infirmities: for we know not what we should pray for as we ought: but the Spirit itself maketh intercession for us with groanings which cannot be uttered. And he that searcheth the hearts knoweth what is the mind of the Spirit, because he maketh intercession for the saints according to the will of God."

The transforming and renewing of my mind that was needed as shown in Romans 12:2 could only happen as I began to delve deeper into God's Word. Here we learn, "..be not conformed to this world; but be ye transformed by the renewing of your mind, that ye may prove what is that good, and acceptable, and perfect will of God." To transform and renew we must be exposed because things just do not transform or renew unless there is exposure to something.

So put your cerebral hemisphere to work and be inquisitive. See what the Word says for yourself. And speaking of the cerebral hemispheres, let's examine them and see how parts of the Head govern the Body.

◆   ◆   ◆

The purpose of this paired mass is to control higher functions such as speech, memory, intelligence, etc.

Soon after I was saved, I had an experience that left me somewhat shaken. I had only been saved a few weeks, and was still not sure how to picture God, except as a loving Person that sent His Son to die for me. I did not know the Bible said God could not lie although I suspected He couldn't. Needless to say I still had some unhealthy fears concerning Him

One day our neighbor came to visit. We'd gone into the kitchen to have some coffee and as he and my husband talked, my husband began to tell him about our salvation. This apparently timid man who would do anything to promote good will in his community, suddenly stood up and raised his voice to my husband. In his anger, he proudly announced that God had never done anything for him. *He* had worked and built his house. *He* had worked and bought his land. *He* had supplied all his family needed, not God. *He* had wealth and no need of anything thanks to the doings of his own two hands.

Even that young in the Lord I knew enough about God not to make remarks like that. It would be some time before I learned to give Him credit for everything I did, but when this man began to discredit God in such a manner, fear gripped me like I had never known. I could picture God throwing a lightning bolt into my kitchen, missing him and hitting me. So I did what any respectable, higher functioning, intelligent mammal would do...I ran.

Since then, I've learned better. But the point is our own head does a very poor job of controlling our intelligence. Our own head does a poor job of controlling our personalities, etc. It was VITAL that God put Jesus as the Head of the Body. Let's examine the function of the Head and see how it relates to us.

6

Your Attitude is Showing

Not only are speech and intelligence listed as higher functions, but so is our personality. I know, I know. You probably are saying most people don't have this higher function because they don't have a personality. But a good one takes time, so be patient. And while you're waiting, try to walk a mile in his shoes before you criticize a man. Then, if he gets angry, you're a mile away and he is barefoot.

The frontal lobe governs our personality. It is located right up front. After all, it is called the frontal lobe. How appropriate that God put it there. Right up front. Right there where everyone would be able to see it. But what are they seeing? What kind of personality are you projecting? It's sad but true that the first impression is usually a lasting impression.

Turn to Galatians 5:22. For a long time I heard people say the *fruits* of the Spirit. But that's not right. It's fruit, without an 'S'. One. Not many. One. Now think about that for a while. I have to admit this had me stumped. There are nine listed. Each one sounds as though it would be tasty to consume. But is it? It should be but you can see by the personalities of a lot of people that they are not eating the fruit.

Let's look at the proverbial apple. The apple is used to explain a lot in the Bible. Adam and Eve? That apple got accused of something it might not have been guilty of. Personally, I think she ate a fig, but that's beside the point. Jacob? God kept him as the apple of His eye. (Zech. 2:8) So we'll use an apple to explain the *fruit*.

You must have three things to have fruit. Roots, trunk or vine, and branches. The Father, Son and Holy Spirit. Now if you pick a fruit from the apple tree you have only one product. Or do you? Let's see.

You have the stem, which kept it on the tree. The pretty green, yellow or red skin, which protects it from the elements. The sweet porous texture of the inside, and of course the seeds, which we use to plant other trees. We picked one fruit, but it contained four parts. Likewise, the fruit of the Spirit. Nine parts, one fruit.

In Galatians 5:19 Paul says that the works of the flesh are manifest and then he goes on to list them. The works of OUR flesh. But notice in verse 22 he does not say the fruit of the Spirit is manifest. This just proves that we all have the sinful nature and it comes quite easily.

Don't get mad. That's what it says. Or does not say. Go down to verse twenty-five and you will understand why it does not say. Read this verse carefully. It's telling us that if we are going to hang on to the tree, at least produce good fruit.

Ever decorate a Christmas tree? When you look it over and you see a bare spot, do you not say, "Put something on this limb…it looks empty?" You have to conscientiously *walk* in the Spirit. There is nothing you can do to live in the Spirit except to ask Jesus to save you from your sins and then "…live according to God in the Spirit." (I Peter 4:6) But you have to work on your spiritual personality. This is not something that is manifested unless there is a little pruning done. You must be willing to completely be led of the Spirit to be able to walk in the Spirit.

This reminds me of a story I heard a long time ago. A preacher had given a series of teachings on the family structure. He emphasized several times the importance of setting a good example. One day, one of the men of his church was walking down the shore of the beach. As he walked, deep in his thoughts, he heard a child giggling behind him. He turned and understanding seeped in. He began to cry as he looked back toward his tracks…tracks that were not always straight but slowed where he had veered off course during his concentration. Tracks that showed where he had stumbled over an obstacle. Tracks that now showed his four year old following in every one, choosing each one so carefully as to place his tiny foot exactly where his daddy's had been.

Tracks that had questioned his ability to be the man he should be. Tracks that had questioned why life seemed so stressed and where is God during all the bad times. Tracks that spoke of alcohol and no time for his family. Tracks that spoke of being the perfect model citizen to the world, but a lonely, scared shell of a man in reality.

Slowly he slipped to his knees and waited for his trusting son to catch up. "Why are you crying, Daddy?" he asked as he wrapped his arms around his father's neck.

"Because you wanted to follow in my footsteps, Son, and I was afraid you might have fallen."

You see, someone is following in our footsteps. Someone is taking the same route we choose to take. Are we being led of the Spirit and following in the Savior's footsteps or those of someone else?

Let's face it. If we didn't have Jesus and His brain as our Head, we couldn't even walk, much less walk in the Spirit. If only we would learn to put these attributes into practice. It's impossible within ourselves to do this, but we can ask the Holy Ghost to teach us how. But be aware that in changing our personality there must be things that happen in order for us to show we have a change.

Personality traits. OK. Between this chapter and another you are going to get real familiar with the fruit of the Spirit, so here goes the first time.

LOVE: One of the Ten Commandments is to love thy neighbor as thy self. (Leviticus 19:18) Have you ever tried to get the people at church together to start a pantry for the needy? Ever really noticed what they bring to eat? Most of the cans are so old and rusty you would think they were fished out of the flood in Noah's day. And it's always something they wouldn't eat themselves. Or try to get them to give clothing to the homeless. You would think the items they choose were made from the fig leaves Adam used to try to cover his sin. No way would they pick out the best, that's always saved for what they consider the less fortunate, which is themselves.

Of course, there's another way to look at that command, and if you do it this way, you can say you actually follow it. Maybe the reason people won't give the best is because they really don't love themselves that much. I see people who suffer from problems that could have been avoided if they had just cared enough to take better care of the body God gave them. So maybe they do give according to how they love themselves, which is very little.

There's another thing with love. I really like Proverbs 10:12. Hatred stirreth up strifes, but love coverth all sins. What's the first thing a Christian will do when someone does something they don't like. Psst, psst, psst, psst. Instead of keeping their mouth shut they have to *telll somebodyyy* or they will just explode. You know, just to get it off their chest. Just 'my best friend' you know, cause they won't tell anybody.

Oh, yeah? What if they don't consider you *their* best friend and decide to tell the one they *do* call best friend? Better yet, what if they decide to tell their husband? Now we know men don't gossip but you never see women sitting on the liar's bench in movies.

JOY: This one cracks me up. Have you ever listened to people when they hear of someone getting a raise or having a very nice vacation? Or when they see the furniture store truck pulling up to deliver a high dollar living room suite? What are the four most spoken words? It's certainly not, "Oh, praise the Lord," or, "I'm happy for you." It's usually, "Humph! Must be nice!"

PEACE: Right. Our personalities just ooze peace. That's why we take medicine for high blood pressure, ulcers, and nerves. Tranquilizers to sleep. Caffeine to wake up. Tablets for our headaches and see counselors like me for our numerous psychosomatic pains. Our pharmacies are getting rich on our abuse of placebos and IT'S LEGAL.

Have you ever just sat and watched people on the streets or in a store? Everyone you see is miserable. Never a smile or taking time just to be pleasant. Never laughing or acting as though they have all the time in the world just to make your day a little brighter. There's no peace on any of the faces.

I enjoy going to my doctor, Dr. Philip Brafford. (Hi, Doc!) And the reason I enjoy it is because he is always saying something that is humorous or related to the Bible. Just recently as I entered his office, he was coming out of an exam room. He smiled and said, "Well, hello, Missy." Then turning to the couple with him, he introduced us and ask if I would show them the Western Wall on the internet. Of course, I was delighted to do this because it gave me a chance to share my Lord with them. We went into his office and began to log on and with each image the excitement grew and we were sharing things that were so uplifting. My tension began to subside and by the time we were finished, I felt I didn't need my physical therapy that day. Of course, I went ahead with it, but the peace this man of God brought to me that day was unreal.

LONG-SUFFERING: I Corinthians 13:4 says it best. "Charity (love) suffereth long, and is kind." One of the favorite sayings of aggravated parents is "I'm through fooling with that child. Let him (or her) do whatever they want."

Now there is such a thing as tough love. Sometimes you have to let someone learn the hard way. But to actually give up on a gift that God has entrusted to you is not, and I repeat, NOT long-suffering. Persistence and consistency in love will prove to be much more rewarding.

Long-suffering is really patience. As parents we loose it a lot of times. We won't usually admit it but the truth is we can get on our children's nerves just as much as they get on ours. They can lose patience, too.

I remember once when our youngest was only about three. He was still having a hard time forming some of his words. But I had been working extra long hours and loosing a lot of sleep. Pressure and stress were heavy. One day he came into the kitchen and asked for a cookie. Instead of simply telling him no I launched into this speech about spoiling his appetite. You know, yada, yada, yada. To a three year old no less. Finally he calmly looked at me and said, "Mommy, you're getting on my nerds." No that's not a typo. He actually said 'nerds'. I guess I need to practice long-suffering.

GENTLENESS: Personality wise a lot of people think this means that a person speaks softly, cries compassionately, and never loses their cool. Not so. My mother-in-law was a very outspoken, frank and to the point person. Yet she was one of the gentlest people I've ever known, and most of the tears she shed were in private.

You would have thought she had a heart of stone in some cases, but through the years I learned better. Her gentle ways would show through with her suddenly calling for the kids for the weekend to give my husband and me a quiet romantic time together, or knowing I had worked all night the night before, she would suddenly appear in my bedroom and gently wake me to a cup of coffee saying, "I know you worked till the crack of dawn, so I turned off your clock, picked the kids up at school and cooked an early dinner. Hope you don't mind." How many women can say their mother-in-law is that gentle?

GOODNESS: One of our granddaughters has a way of making me feel like a dog and she doesn't even know it. She apparently hates math, although I don't think she would admit it. I can chew her out for not studying and send her to the corner to contemplate. But before the day is over she will run up to me, hug my neck and say, "I love you, Nanny. You're so good." Kids have a way of cutting you in two, you know. I would say this kid has more goodness in her than I do, wouldn't you?

FAITH: Now how can faith be a part of a person's personality? Easy. Actually, this should be the most endearing personality trait for a Christian. Faith is our secret weapon. When the world is coming apart at the seams, we can sit back and gloat with a smile on our face because we KNOW things are going to work out. And one of the best ways to antagonize someone is to constantly be smiling in the midst of turmoil. Makes 'em wonder what you're up to.

Speaking of faith reminds me. Can an atheist get insurance for acts of God?

You see, our faith takes on an entirely different attire when faced with catastrophe. And why do we only implore our acts of faith during a crisis? Why not something beautiful and exciting? God enjoys making us happy, too...not just getting us out of trouble.

MEEKNESS: You would think meekness and gentleness are the same. But it's not. 'Chrestotes' is the Greek word for gentleness and it means kindness or usefulness. That's what my mother-in-law was because after all the time I spent in school, working and trying to raise a family, I found her actions very gentle. Meekness on the other hand uses the word 'praotes' which means mildness. Now I ask you, if you were tired and someone came in to help because they knew you were tired, which would you rather have…usefulness or mildness? Usefulness gets the job done. Mildness on the other hand, sympathizes while it's being done.

Also, being meek doesn't mean you have to be a doormat. Numbers 12:3 says, "Now the man Moses was very meek…" But he didn't let people get by with every thing. Notice the difference here. This passage is relating how his brother and sister had verbally attacked him for marrying an Ethiopian woman. They didn't approve. God was infuriated. So He struck Miriam with leprosy. Moses was meek about the whole thing and asked God not to lay the sin to her charge, to forgive her. She had just gossiped about his wife and like any man should do, he should have really let her have it and defended his wife…but no. He was meek. However…

When it came to the people making and worshipping the golden calf in Exodus 32, Moses became a different person. In verse 19 of chapter 32 we read, "And it came to pass, as soon as he came high unto the camp. That he saw the calf, and the dancing: and MOSES' ANGER WAXED HOT, and he cast the tables out of his hands and broke them beneath the mount." (Capitalization added)

Now why was he so meek when Miriam and Aaron ran their mouths, and not so meek when he saw the golden calf?

I think the key word here in understanding the difference, would be the hypocrisy of the people. The difference here is when Miriam and Aaron verbally attacked Moses, they were only questioning his position due to jealousy and the obvious dislike of his spouse. Moses was a humble man when it came to people's ignorance and he took it with fortitude and humility, letting them speak their thoughts and then asking God to forgive them. But when the dude came down from the mountain and saw the people open and blatantly worshipping the calf, he was furious because they had used God to obtain every thing they wanted, but still did not want to worship Him. I think in reality he was saying, "Pick on me all you want. I'm just as guilty as you and I must remember that. But when you pick on my Lord, it means war!"

Being meek doesn't mean you let people run over you but there is a way to fight back. And that is by asking God to help them. But when the Body starts dancing around the golden calf, then it's time to speak up and demand that they stop. "What can we do," you ask. Simple.

One woman opened a keg of nails on abortion and we allowed it by not speaking up. And those that did, didn't fight long enough. One woman got prayer taken out of school and we allowed it by not speaking up. And those that did, did not fight long enough. We should remind our representative that we put them in office and we can take them out. One teen in Baghdad, Arizona wrote how she felt about silence and although it was a teen, this young person show more compassion, backbone, and foresight than most of the people that's been Christians for many years. This is a new school prayer that should be in every classroom, every court, and every home. Although I don't know your name so I can give you credit where it is due, if by any chance you ever read this, my hat goes off to you and in my eyes, you are more courageous than most adults. The poem reads:

Now I sit me down in school, where praying is against the rule.

For this great nation under God, finds mention of Him very odd.

If scripture now the class recites, it violates the Bill of Rights.

And any time my head I bow becomes a Federal matter now.

Our hair can be purple, orange or green. That's no offense; it's a freedom scene.

The law is specific, the law is precise, Prayers spoken aloud are a serious vice.

For praying in public hall might offend someone with no faith at all.

In silence alone we must meditate. God's name is prohibited by the State.

We're allowed to cuss and dress like freaks, pierce our noses, tongues and cheeks.

They've outlawed guns, but first the Bible. To quote the Good Book makes me liable

We can elect a pregnant Senior Queen, and the 'unwed daddy' our Senior King.

It's inappropriate to teach right from wrong. We're taught such judgments do not belong

We can get our condoms and birth controls, study witchcraft, vampires and totem poles.

But the Ten Commandments are not allowed. No word of God must reach this crowd

It's scary here I must confess, when chaos reigns the school's a mess.

So, Lord, this silent plea I make:

Should I get shot, my soul please take! Amen.

Paints a lovely picture of what our youth is feeling, doesn't it? It looks as though the one that wrote this has learned how to do what is says in Colossians 3:12 where it reads, "Put on therefore, as the elect of God, holy and beloved, bowels of mercies, kindness, humbleness of mind, MEEKNESS, long-suffering..." (Capitalization added) Wow! We are supposed to put it on as one would clothing. And wear it, no less! And I would think this person knows the difference between being meek and gentle.

TEMPERANCE: Self-restraint. How is that a personality trait? Well, most people that exercise self-restraint are almost always mild natured and can get along with anyone. So many times I've heard this in the context of moderate drinking. (Which, by the way, makes me wonder why some denominations won't have a teacher that smokes but will have one that is a *moderate* weight of three hundred pounds or a singer that has their nerve pills refilled every thirty days for the last five years. Does this make sense? I'm not advocating nicotine but let's be reasonable and not ride hobbyhorses.)

Anyway, one of the most beautiful portraits of temperance I've ever seen was one of a wife to a man that had been previously married. We'll call the first one 'wife A' and the second 'wife B'. It seems there came a day when wife B, who shows all the parts of the fruit of the Spirit, needed to speak to wife A concerning visitation and transportation with the children for the weekend.

Wife A was so sarcastic to wife B that she finally had to hang up...in tears. Upon witnessing this behavior between good and evil (wife B was using my phone) I thought to myself, "Wife B is a lot better person than I am. I wouldn't have shown that much self-restraint."

If you read Galatians 5:19-21 you will see the personality traits of a person that is not serving Christ. Since the words in verse twenty-one reads, "and such like...' it seems that between the two different kinds of traits, there is more than twenty-seven traits. Would it not be better to choose the last nine instead of the first eighteen? I hear Christians saying all the time how tired they are. Maybe it's because they work themselves to death. Why not take the easy way out and only perform nine feats instead of eighteen?

But as Paul plainly tells us, we are still in the flesh and to show forth the attributes of the Holy Ghost is extremely hard. In Romans 7: 18-20 he is in a miserable state...just realizing that even he can't live the way we are suppose to live. "For I know that in me, (that is, in my flesh) dwelleth no good thing: for to will is present with me; but how to perform that which is good I find not. For the good that I would I do not, but the evil which I would not, that I do. Now if I do that I would not, it is no more I that do it, but sin that dwelleth in me."

And in verse twenty-four, actually cries out for someone to deliver him from this vile earthly tabernacle. "Oh, wretched man that I am! Who shall deliver me from the body of this death?"

Since the works of the flesh are manifested, it is a natural thing. But since we are supposed to put on (or get dressed in) the works of the Spirit such as meekness, this putting on would indicate we are to cover our ugly nakedness of the flesh and choose garments of righteousness. To put something on involves making a decision and performing an action. It is a conscious thought followed by movement. The only ones that do not make this decision for themselves are infants. Someone must cover the nakedness for a child until he or she is capable of doing it for themselves. However, in the Body, most people want to remain in the nudist colonies and continue being naked and their personalities show it.

That's why God chose to make Jesus the Head…ours doesn't act right.

7

And He Was Not

Another part of the cerebral hemispheres is the motor cortex or voluntary movement. Our bodies have supportive framework that allows flexibility of movement. All movement of the body is carried out by muscles, and these muscles are able to do their job because they are made up of tissues that can contract.

There are two categories of muscles. The first one is the voluntary muscles, such as those in the arms and legs that are under conscious control and will contract only when your brain tells them to. An example of this would be if you want to bend your elbow, (and this usually works well when eating) your brain tells your biceps to contract.

To straighten the arm (I guess this is so you can chew better) your brain tells the biceps to chill out or relax and instructs the triceps to contract. All this communication is done via your nervous system. Imagine all this talking and we didn't even hear the phone ring.

The second category is the involuntary muscles. This includes those that are in the heart and digestive tract. These usually function without awareness (unless you have heartburn) or conscious control. Since we are looking at the part of the brain that controls voluntary movement I suppose we should ignore the second part, for now anyway.

Walking is something you have to think about. It is a voluntary movement. Now this thinking doesn't necessarily have to be a long-term meditation or even involve losing much needed sleep. If you want to walk to the refrigerator and there's nothing wrong with you physically, just think glass of cold tea and voila! Your legs will get up and go, taking the rest of your body with them You see, your legs always associates tea and walking together, but nevertheless, you must think first. Once in my grandchild's classroom there were three posters in bright bold colors. The posters said "Listen, think, do." The same principle applies here.

Let's use walking as one of the voluntary movements. Ever paid any attention to a person taking a hike on a mountainous trail? As they start uphill they are

usually standing upright. As the incline becomes steeper they gradually start leaning forward just a tad until finally they are almost bent double. Their steps start
out sure and strong, gradually becoming a clomp! instead of a spring. By the time
they reach the halfway point their legs are having a hard time interpreting the
message coming from the brain and they lift their legs as though they suddenly
gained fifty pounds.

Going down is a different story entirely. The steps are no longer slow and
strained. In fact, it's quite comical. Steps can be sure but the body is leaning
backward. At least until gravity kicks in, then it's a choice of either run or roll.

The point is voluntary movement can be quite hard at times. Especially walking. This could even be scary if we weren't aware of the fact that Jesus is coming
back for us and there will be such a thing as the rapture or catching away to be
with Him in the air. After all, look at Enoch. The Bible says in Genesis 5:24 that,
"Enoch walked with God; and he was not: for God took him." Took him where?
Now we know he was taken to heaven but how would a new Christian react to
this if they did not know about the rapture? And don't take for granted all Christians know about the rapture.

What's it like to walk with God? Well, Deuteronomy 5:33 pretty much puts it
this way…walk the way He tells us to walk and you'll live and things will be well.
See, walking is a choice, a decision to be made. God told the Israelites in Deuteronomy 30:19. "…I have set before you life and death, blessing and cursing,
therefore choose life that both thou and thy seed may live."

But a baby needs to be taught how to walk. That's why you see people holding
babies' hands a lot when they start walking. Just like us. We not only need God
holding our hand and teaching us how to walk but where to walk. I Kings 8:36
says, "Then hear thou in heaven and forgive the sin of thy servants, and of thy
people Israel, that thou *teach* them the good way wherein they should walk…"
(Italics added)

But please understand that since Christ is the Head and we are the Body, you
can rest assured that the Body as a whole will walk the way He wants us to. And
Romans 8:1 tells us how to walk, "…after the Spirit." Why must we walk this
way? Verse four explains it nicely. "…that the righteousness of the law might be
fulfilled in us who walk not after the flesh, but after the Spirit."

There are several ways to walk written in the Bible. We can walk according to
His commands as in Psalms 1 or in His ways according to Joshua 22:5. We can
walk uprightly as in Proverbs 2:7 and in His statues and judgments as in Ezekiel
37:24. We can walk in the newness of life in Romans 6:4 and after the Spirit in
Roman 8:1. We can walk honestly as in the day in Romans 13:13 and by faith in

II Corinthians 5:7. We can walk in love in Ephesians 5:2 and worthy of the Lord in Colossians 1:10. We can walk by the gospel rule in Philippians 3:16 and in the light in I John 1:7. Last of all, and simply glorious is, we can walk in white raiment as in Revelations 3:4 and in the light of heaven as in Revelation 21:24. And I can't think of any thing that is the light of heaven but Jesus Christ Himself, and since we're His Body, guess who will shine if they walk right?

Standing…this is a voluntary movement the physical body finds hard to do. Standing is extremely hard for people with arthritic knees. The motor cortex deals with the movement of the muscles, but some of those muscles would not be worth anything if they did not have the skeletal system inside them. It would be so nice if the Body of Christ would realize how badly we need each other, and stop turning our noses up at other people or denominations. Just because a Baptist or Pentecostal doesn't do the same function doesn't mean they are not a part of the Body. Just because muscles and bones do not function in the same capacity, doesn't mean you don't need both. So, back to standing.

Voluntary movement must be thought about first. Your body doesn't just suddenly stand after sitting. If it did, and you weren't planning it, or something didn't go through your mind to make it react, then something is badly wrong! It would be like the song performed by Ray Stevens where he said he quit sitting up with the dead since the dead started sitting up, too. But let's presume that we are sitting and we've decided to stand. I want you to pay close attention to the sequence of events here.

Sitting implies a relaxed position. All of the weight of the body is placed on one area and we won't mention the name of that area. But in performing the act of sitting, one has taken the load off the feet and legs, giving them a chance to rest. Now this relaxed, restful position seems like such a relief to most of us. But in some cases, like a person that is extremely overweight, this can be a relatively bad position especially when used a lot. When a person is overweight and sitting, they may be relaxed but it is actually causing harm to the body, because it interferes with circulation, resulting in an accumulation of fluid in the lower extremities, or the ankles and feet. This is one of the things a doctor will watch for with people who have congestive heart failure. So sitting, for some, can be dangerous.

The Bible says in Amos 6:1, "woe to them that are at ease in Zion and trust in the mountain of Samaria, which are named chief of the nations, to whom the house of Israel came!" The word 'ease' in this passage means rest and the word 'Zion' means fort or fortress. So the passage could read, "Woe to them that are at rest in the fortress…"

When there is a war or the possibility of battle, the ones inside the fort should be constantly preparing and on guard. Making ready the weapons, securing sites of possible entry, and observing the surrounding area are all necessary actions of defense. One must stand to perform all these actions. We are in a perpetual war until the Messiah returns and those of us that are sitting with ease in our salvation are the ones that pose the most danger. Are we our brother's keeper? Yes! Ezekiel 33:1-9 seems to make this very clear. (I guess you have learned by now that you can't read my books unless you have a Bible handy, so go get it and look it up.)

So if the Body sits too much we have an accumulation of fluid. The Body shouldn't get to relaxed. Instead, it should let the thought pass through the mind to the motor cortex that we need to move.

Standing is the next step. Everyone knows a baby must learn to stand before it can walk. That applies to everyone. Standing involves a locking of the joints in the knees, a definite pulling together of muscle and bone and then a stubborn refusal to bend, thus placing the body in an upright position.

There is a clear picture in Exodus 14:13 where we see how God has instructed the Body to stand with the two denominations of muscle and bone pulling together. It reads, "...stand still, and see the salvation of the Lord..." This is a clear picture of the Jews and Gentiles alike being in the Body and having salvation extended to them. Don't forget we have already mentioned the multitude was mixed. Check Exodus 12:37, 38. This is just after the death angel passed over and the children were allowed to leave Egypt. The journey is just beginning and it says the multitude was mixed.

Since there are only two categories of people in the Bible, Jews and Gentiles, I would think the words mixed multitude meant both categories. So the muscles and bones were pulling together when the statement was made, "...stand still and see the salvation of the Lord."

In Psalms 89 we see where God made an agreement with David. The entire psalm is thrilling but the promise He made in verse 28 shows us that not only will He stand with us, but we can rest assured by this promise, He will enable the Body to stand as well. The promise is "My mercy will I keep for him forevermore and my covenant shall *stand fast with him.*" (Italics added) We can stop sitting and stand upright with this promise.

In Proverbs 12:7 we see that the promise is even more secure. "The wicked are overthrown, and are not: but the house of the righteous shall stand." So even if we have bad knees we can still stand.

Of course, trying to stand without our Brain telling us to can be quite humiliating. For instance, in Proverbs 25: 6,7 it says, "Put not forth thyself in the presence of the king, and stand not in the place of great men: For better it is that it be said unto thee, "Come up hither," than that thou shouldest be put lower in the presence of the prince whom thine have seen."

In Romans 14:4 we see that even though we have problems with the knees God is able to make us stand. "…he shall be holden up, for God is able to make him stand."

We always want to stand on even ground so as not to fall and I Corinthians 2:5 tells us how. "That your faith should not stand in the wisdom of men, but in the power of God."

There are many reasons our bodies will stand. If we have been sitting to long; if there are no available seats, if we are performing certain tasks; if we are getting ready to move as in walking, or if we are sitting and suddenly want a glass of tea. (I guess you can tell by now that I like tea, but this makes me stand a lot.) But the best reason is because we have been chosen of God to salvation through sanctification of the Spirit and belief of the truth…because we have been called. So we see in II Thessalonians 2:15, "Therefore, brethren, stand fast, and hold the traditions which you have been taught, whether by word, or our epistle."

I really enjoy knowing of an upcoming battle and the Body's Head tells us how to get ready for it. Ephesians 6:10-18 is not boot camp; it's full-fledged war.

"Finally, my brethren, be strong in the Lord, and in the power of his might. Put on the whole armor of God, they ye may be able to *stand* against the wiles of the devil. For we wrestle not against flesh and blood, but against principalities, against powers, against the rulers of the darkness of this world, against spiritual wickedness in high places. Wherefore take unto you the whole armor of God that ye may be able to with*stand* in the evil day, and having done all, to *stand*. *Stand* therefore, having your loins girt about with truth, and having on the breastplate of righteousness; and your feet shod with the preparation of the gospel of peace; Above all, taking the shield of faith, wherewith ye shall be able to quench all the fiery darts of the wicked. And take the helmet of salvation, and the sword of the Spirit, which is the word of God; Praying always with all prayer and supplication in the Spirit and watching thereunto with all perseverance and supplication for all saints."

After reading all the things we are instructed to wear, I would say God is warning us not to stand without getting dressed first. It would make the Body more susceptible to the elements. And if the Body is supposed to dress before it stands, you would soon realize that sitting and being at ease with all that armor would not be so relaxing after a while. The Body as a whole will have a day of rest and relaxation soon. (Hebrews 4) In the meantime, listen to your motor cortex and *Stand.*

◆   ◆   ◆

Another part controlled by the motor cortex is the hands. Hands are so useful, don't you think? Most of us eat with them, we motion with them when we talk, we use them to bop the dog on the nose with a newspaper, and most importantly, we use them to scratch an itch that is driving us crazy in the middle of the night. But did you know the hands have a much better job to do, one that you don't see many parents or grandparents doing? On July 17, 1997 my husband and I stood in the hall of the hospital, right in front of the large window that showed a door leading to an operating room. After what seemed like an eternity, but in reality was only a few minutes, the door opened and our youngest son walked through carrying a small, wrinkled, red-haired angry boy, our grandson.

As Joe laid the loudest part of the baby's body (his mouth) down into the bassinet, making sure the rest of the body followed equally as safely, the nurse looked through the window, smiled and said, "You may come in and hold the baby, if you like."

If I like!! I like, I like. "One at a time, please," I said. Putting my motor cortex into operation, and using my hands to shove my husband aside, through the door my legs went, also with the aid of my motor cortex.

Tears in my eyes and an awesome feeling in my heart, I couldn't help but be amazed at yet another perfect creation of my Lord, although I did wonder if God had a reason for his lungs being so strong and containing such volume. But his little face was so cute, even wrinkled in anger.

By this time in my Christian growth I had learned what my hands were really designed for, so, every so gently, I picked him up, introduced myself, and holding him in one arm and laying my other hand on his head, I spoke a blessing on him. The blessing was that he would be used of God to spread the gospel and always have compassion for his fellow man. Of course, now that he is older and *all boy*, as they used to say, it may appear that the blessing did not take. But it did and he will. I know the Bible says to have faith, but come on Lord. Didn't You also say You wouldn't put more on us than we could bear?

Genesis 48:14-20 gives an account of Jacob blessing his children right before he died. When will Christians realize their hands can do more than slap a kid, that they have power in those hands to impart a beautiful blessing instead?

In Numbers 8:10 we see a perfect picture of ordaining someone to the Lord. And what did they do? They laid hands on them. Most people today use their hands to pick up the phone and relate all the faults of another, thereby sowing seeds of discord. And the only way they want to lay hands on the brethren is fast, hard and continuously.

Did you know you have the power in your hands to impart healing? Jesus did in Mark 6:5 and Paul did in Acts 28:8. But that was Jesus and Paul, you might argue. So? Use your hands and turn to Mark 16:18.

One thing I never could understand is why preachers always quote Mark 16:15 and go on and on about the great commission of preaching to the lost, and forget the rest about the signs that shall follow them that believe.

In speaking to a ladies' ministry one night, my topic was 'Where Are the Signs?' This goes a little deeper than most preachers want to admit and we need to put the cerebral hemispheres in action for the higher functions and think about the fact that Jesus said, "…and greater works than these shall ye do…" And He raised the dead!! You can't get any greater with your hands.

I really like the action concerning the use of the hands found in I Kings 18:30-40. The first thing a Christian should do in showing the world that Jesus is Lord is to use their hands to repair the altar of the Lord that's been broken down. When you are over powered by the world, hit the altar and confess your weakness because that is when you become strong. Dig deep into your heart and get ready. Next you need to put every thing in order. Then you should give wholeheartedly out of your need.

Elijah had the men use twelve barrels of water to saturate the altar. They must have really thought he was nuts because there was a severe draught. What's the first thing people say when it's time to give to someone in need or even pay their tithes? "I need it myself." By looking at their own draught, they haven't saturated the altar. Last of all, clap your hands in praise when blessings come.

My favorite use of the hands is found in Matthew 27:32-56. You will need to read it completely to understand why I humbly say, "It wasn't my motor cortex that told the legs on the Man of Matthew 27:32-56 to climb Calvary's hill. It wasn't my motor cortex that extended those hands. It wasn't my motor cortex that caused all the muscles to move voluntarily to come up out of the grave. It was the One that holds all the fullness of the Godhead.

But it was my motor cortex that told my hand to reach up and take hold of the hand that was scarred for me. And my hand did.

8

Open Your Mouth and Say, "Ahh"

Ecclesiastes 3:7 says there is a time to be silent and a time to speak.

We were blessed with our first grandchild in the fall of 1989. As time moved on, she made the appropriate goo-goo sounds that all babies make. We laughed with joy and gave encouraging words as our son asked, "Mom, when will she ever start talking?"

She was curious and full of life, eager to learn and always exploring. She was five and beautiful. Finally, the day arrived when our son asked, "Mom, when will she ever hush?"

The speech center is located up front to the left, right next to the frontal lobe, which governs our personality. Do you think it odd that the Lord would put these two governing centers side by side? Not really. Turn with me to Matthew 12:34-37. And I quote:

"O generation of vipers, how can ye, being evil, speak good things? For out of the abundance of the heart the mouth speaketh. A good man out of the good treasure of the heart bringeth forth evil things. But I say unto you, That every idle word that men shall speak, they shall give account thereof in the day of judgment."

In studying this text, we see the Lord is cautioning us about our words. Remember He is the Head. We are the Body and made in His likeness. We know He was sinless and never spoke idle or unprofitable words. There are several scriptures that caution us on our mouth and the use of our words. Let's look at these.

Proverbs 29:20 says, "Seest thou a man that is hasty in his words? There is more hope of a fool than of him." WOW! That's heavy. The Bible says in Psalms 14:1 and Psalms 53:1 that a fool has said in his heart there is no God. So I guess that puts the speech center of an atheist in the heart. Most people really feel that an atheist has no hope. But look carefully at the difference of Proverbs 29:20 and

Psalms 14:1. There is more hope of a fool than someone that is hasty in his words. How many Christians do we know that shoot off their mouth before putting it in gear?

Why is this true? Well, the word fool in the references in Psalms means 'empty'. Of course, a fool couldn't be any other way since the life is in the blood and a fool hasn't had the blood applied. And the word fool in Proverbs means self-confident. He's putting his confidence in himself instead of God. Self-confident instead of God-confident. Matthew 12:34 tells us, "...out of the abundance of the heart the mouth speaketh." The word abundance means superfluity, or excess, oversupply.

So we have a person speaking the abundance of his heart, which is nothing. Do you know what an atheist is? It's a non-*prophet* organization.

Have you ever been around people that only speak misery? I know a person that will speak negatively about everything. I mean the sky can be a Carolina blue from one end of the earth to the other and if you comment on its beauty, she will say, "Yeah, it's pretty, but it won't stay that way. My arthritis says it's going to rain." She is the type that will put a sign on the office door saying tomorrow has been cancelled due to lack of interest. A doctor once gave this person a 95% chance of total recovery and when it was retold, it was with sadness that he only gave her a 95% recovery rate.

HEY! If I was seventy years old and something was wrong that prevented me from doing anything, and I got a 95% recovery rate, I'd be ecstatic and take my chances. But some people enjoy being miserable and if you talk to them very long you become miserable, too. Why?

Our five senses are there for a purpose. When we use them all, we have a sixth sense. It's called common sense. In Mark 4:24 we are told to "...take heed what you hear." In order to hear something the noise or sound must first be made. That is usually a spoken sound. We need to remove ourselves from these situations or get a Holy Ghost boldness about us and start rebuking the one speaking.

I don't want an abundance of some one else's misery in my heart so that I speak foolishness. That's why God put our speaking center next to our personality center. He was hoping it would influence it. He even gave us the tools to use in Galatians 5:22 that would influence our speaking. Let's face it. If Jesus wasn't our Head and if His speech center was not next to His personality, we'd be in a heap of trouble.

Have you ever heard the expression 'you talk too much'? I learned a long time ago that when someone starts giving me a lot of compliments, I'd better watch out. So many times in my life I have been around people that seem to constantly say bad things or find fault with someone else. And with each negative remark it is usually followed by, "Now I'm not speaking of you, you know that. You are one of the best and if you ever need anything, anything at all, just let me know. Why, I would give my life for you." And I know that for everyone these people talk about, they usually are saying the same thing about me to them. It's just common sense.

We have a very dear friend that stayed with us during his medical training. He is from Korea. We grew to care for him deeply and he was given liberty to anything in our home but you would never know the boy was there unless you see him. So quiet and respectful. He felt at ease and knew he wass welcome and I think he enjoyed being here. He hardly ever speaks but when he does…

Well, let me put it this way. I've never caught him in a lie, not even a little white one. Which reminds me. Who ever thought of painting lies white? I've never seen him knowingly take advantage of anyone or anything and when he does give a compliment, it is short and to the point. There is no rattling on and on. He simply says things like, "Thank you, ma'am. Dinner was good," or "May I help you with the dishes?" His words aren't useless or constant. But his eyes show the tender way he feels about people when he cares.

The world could learn something from him because he doesn't always feel he has to keep up a barrage of speech. His speech is nowhere near excessive. And that is what the Lord was talking about in Proverbs 10:8, 19. Verse 8 reads, "the wise in heart will receive commandments: but a prating fool shall fall."

The word prating means trifling or empty talk, a sound that is meaningless, repetitive, and suggestive of the chatter of children. Have you ever heard people that talk all the time but never say anything? Endless chatter but never having a point. Never saying anything that will help someone to grow or increase his or her knowledge or wisdom. Through the years I've learned to tune these people out.

Verse 19 is even better. "In the multitude of words there wanteth not sin: but he that refraineth his lips is wise."

He that refraineth his lips is wise. In other words, keep your mouth shut. I challenge every one of you to practice this instruction for one day. Just try it. You would be surprised at the difference. This prevents a lot of 'he said, she said', that can come back to haunt you.

My friend and I were talking one day of how the Body is constantly feeling sorry for itself, and constantly voicing its sorrow. We in America have it so rough. The people overseas don't have the foggiest clue as to what rough is. Some of the ways we have it rough are obvious and no one around the world wants to help us.

How do we have it so rough? Well, let's look and see and it must be true because we hear the Body voicing its complaints all the time.

We have it rough by the amount of food we have. Other countries are just starving to death while we in America have to burn up a thousand calories a day just trying to decide whether to go back for seconds or not. I've lost five pounds just thinking about it.

We also have it rough because we have a church on every corner and if we are a member of one, the pastor actually expects us to attend. And that's on Sunday, our only day off. And to make matters worse, the pastor expects us to give a tithe and offering so he can get paid out of our hard earned money. Whereas the other countries only have to find a hidden cave or basement in order to worship in secrecy so they won't get their heads chopped off. And if the people don't show up for service, then the pastor only has to worry whether they are still alive or not. How dare the other countries think we have it so easy?

Why just the other day someone I know had to get her washing machine fixed. A belt had broken on it and she couldn't even buy a new machine. She actually had to be satisfied with a new belt. And the people overseas washing in the nasty rivers think they have it rough.

Some of us even work eight hours a day and then have to come home to our air conditioning and cook dinner for the family. And the ones overseas think because they have to sit outside in the sun with no food at all and watch their children with their swollen abdomens begging for something to eat, that we have it made. How dare they think America is easy?

Actually, America needs to wake up and frankly, I feel we need to do without a few things. I'm not talking about whether to cook chicken or steak. I'm talking about fasting a while. Some of us need it.

Our words have such impact. Try to picture in your mind a word taking shape in your mouth. I don't mean shaping as in the rolling of the tongue and lips together to form a word. I mean the word actually taking on a form such as you see in the comic strips. The words there are usually pictured inside a big bubble extending from the mouth of the one speaking.

Each one of us has had the experience of speaking to someone that has great enthusiasm about something. Their speech is vibrant, their steps are bouncy, and their whole body language is exciting. Then someone opens his mouth in a negative way and you can see the shoulders begin to sag, the voice take on a different tone and before long, this person is nodding his or her head in agreement with all the negative thinking. It's as though the negative words took the shape of a bowling ball and knocked down all the words that once excited him.

Jesus told His disciples that if any part of the body offended another part, to cut it off. It would be better to go into Heaven maimed than go to hell whole. Makes you wonder how many that was grafted into the Body of Christ become offensive. Makes you wonder even more about the 'good, Godly people' that suffer a premature death. What were they speaking? It's thoughts such as these that make me ever so glad that Jesus is the Head of our whole Body...of every Christian. This could even go so far as to mean some of us need to cut out our tongue. A lot of people have a tongue that is tied in the middle and loose on both ends.

Jesus has all the fruit of the Spirit and He doesn't speak us into trouble, but most of the trouble that comes our way is from our own mouth. The three monkeys had it right when they said, "See no evil, hear no evil, speak no evil." Who ever thought of that must have taken God at His word and realized how our senses influence our actions and he probably lived a long life.

Most people think our mouths are for eating only. If we could just grasp the importance of our words. If we could only put our brain in gear before we do our mouth. Jesus defeated the devil with words. Not weapons or His fists. Words. Words are so powerful.

Let's have a little English lesson here. Do you remember the game we played as children, "Mother may I?" All the kids would line up and one person would be the mother. She would give a command to someone in line to perform a certain task such as taking three giant steps. Who ever got to the mother first by performing the commands was the winner but they could only perform the commands with permission from the mother. Every time a command was given, they were to respond by asking, "Mother, may I?" If the mother said, "Yes, you may," then you proceeded. If she said, "No, you may not," then you remained where you were.

Now think back to your English classes in school. The teacher would explain the proper times to use certain words such as neither, nor and either, or. One set of words was may and can. You are to use the word can when showing you are capable of performing a certain act. You are to use the word may to show that you might actually do it or in asking permission. When playing the game it is improper to say, "Mother, can I?" because everyone knew you were capable of taking three giant steps. But you were to ask permission before you actually performed the task. Thus, "Mother *may* I?"

Understanding this, now get your Bible and turn to I Peter 5:8. It reads, "Be sober, be vigilant, because your adversary the devil, as a roaring lion, walketh about, seeking whom he *may* devour." (Italics added)

Look at that!! "…whom he MAY devour." You have to give the joker permission first. He can't touch you unless you let him and when you open your mouth in a negative way, you are speaking *against* the scriptures and giving your permission.

Have you ever talked to someone that was hurt by words years ago? It's hard for them to forget what was said. Once words are spoken they are impossible to take back. The pain lingers on and on. People can say what they want, but the fact remains that the Bible tells us that out of the abundance of our hearts the mouth speaks. So when someone says something in anger, rest assured they meant it. It was in their heart. They can say, "I didn't mean it," all they want, but they did. Maybe they didn't mean that they felt that way all the time because the heart can hold an abundance of things. Nevertheless, at the *time* it was said, it was meant.

I would love to have been there when Jesus told old slew-foot "…it is written, Man shall not live by bread alone, but by every word that proceedeth out of the mouth of God." Most people today go to church to get fed…literally. More time is spent on meat, vegetables, and banana pudding than on the word. People think God leaves the church at twelve and goes to Kentucky Fried Chicken.

John 6:63 is one of the most beautiful verses in the Bible. Let me take the time to quote it to you. "It is the Spirit that quickeneth; the flesh profiteth nothing; the *words* that I speak unto you, *they* are Spirit and *they* are life." (Italics added) It's the Words!! Man, that's awesome. The words are life and the life is in the blood.

Did you ever stop to think that you can't even live without God speaking it? Did you ever stop to think that most of the things we say to our children have an adverse affect on them? Ever listen to a parent yelling at their kids, "You'll never amount to anything!" or "I don't have time to mess with you now," and then conveniently forgetting when they do have time?

Some people really make me see red. All you can hear is, "I want a baby, I want a baby." They finally get their baby and then when it's bottle time, or fever time, or getting up early time, or helping with school work time, or better yet, teaching them Christ time, their words change dramatically.

I recently had the privilege of home-schooling three of our grandchildren, the eldest, Jaimie, picked up a habit that thrills me. When one of them had done something they shouldn't do, it was my duty during school time to reprimand. One of my favorite ways was to start out by saying, "The Bible says…"

Jaimie has become so interested in the Word that no matter what she is doing, she will stop and say, "Wait, I want to hear this." Of course, there are always scriptures we can speak to enhance our lives and gain victory. For instance, Isaiah 54:17 tells us no weapon formed against us shall prosper. This verse literally saved a man's life when he was at the gunpoint of a raving lunatic. He kept repeating this verse and every shot that was fired missed him. He was at point blank range. If you have never heard Pastor John Hagee of Cornerstone Church in San Antonia, Texas give his testimony about this incident, you need to, because it will amaze you.

Repeat after me: "Lord, from this day forward, I want my speech center in line and complete obedience to the Head of my Body. Beginning today, help me to only speak in love, joy, peace, long-suffering, gentleness, faith, meekness, and temperance. In Jesus' name.

At this point, I'd like to recommend a book for you. It is *'The Tongue, A Creative Force'* and it was written by Charles Capps. This book will open your eyes to a lot of things that will prove to you how the Body has been programmed to speak destructive things on Itself and It is literally trying not to receive what the Head is telling It. This book will make you stop and pay attention to everything you say if you let the Spirit guide you.

Remember in the previous chapter we ask about how tasty the fruit can be? It's hard to swallow at first on a lot of things, but the results and change are tremendous.

This takes practice. Speaking in love is hard when you've just discovered your neighbor has stolen your car. Speaking in joy is almost impossible when you find out your mother-in-law if moving in. (Why would people have a problem with that anyway…men or women?) Peace is difficult when you know the rent is due tomorrow and your checkbook is made of rubber. Long-suffering turns to nerve pills when your teenager keeps getting speeding tickets and he is on your insurance.

Gentleness goes out the window when you have to keep picking up your husband's socks. Goodness can't even survive when the only time people visit is if they want to borrow money. Speaking faith is hard when you keep entering those sweepstakes and each year somebody else wins. (I'm not talking lottery now.) Meekness must indicate people think you are a coward when they keep putting you in sticky situations and you refrain from saying anything. And my favorite is temperance. I mean how can you speak no to seconds for pecan pie? Surely there must be an exception to temperance at such occasions as Christmas, Thanksgiving, birthdays, reunions, Yom Kippur, Hanukkah, Veteran's Day, Columbus Day…you get the picture. OK. Temperance is one I need to work on.

My husband used to have a favorite saying when our boys talked too much. It seemed there was a song by Simon and Garfunkel years ago entitled, *'Silence is Golden'*. Every time our boys talked unceasingly my husband would raise his voice just a little over theirs and say, "Silence is golden, so be quiet and get rich."

Speaking of speaking…you know most of the time it's the women that get blamed for talking too much. Due to this, a preacher once told me he could take the Bible and prove that women were not going to heaven. There would be no women there at all. He then told me to look at Revelations 8:1. In this verse John says that when the seventh seal was opened, there was silence in heaven about the space of half an hour. Any time you have silence that long, you can rest assured a woman is not present.

Of course, he told me this at a time when we were visiting and it was supposed to be cute and entertaining. But one thing I noticed was his wife was very quiet, (she hardly had a chance to speak) and was constantly doing things to make our visit enjoyable while he just sat there and *talked*.

Our words have destiny. Our words can influence God. Moses influenced God with his words after God became angry with the spies that were sent into Canaan and came back with a bad report. God was going to kill them but Moses petitioned Him and influenced Him with his words. In Numbers 14:20 we read, "And the Lord said, I have pardoned *according to thy word.'* (Italics added)

I've heard so many people ask, "Why would a loving God send someone to hell?" I think Matthew 12:37 pretty much explains it. We condemn our own selves by our words. This is so evident because in Romans 10:9 Paul writes, "That if thou shalt *confess with thy mouth* the Lord, Jesus, and shalt believe in thine heart that God hath raised him from the dead, thou shalt be saved." (Italics added) Your words of confession are powerful. For most people, having the gift of 'speaking in tongues' is dangerous. It's called the gift of gab.

Another thing that really riles me is how people will constantly speak badly of their employer, or better yet, our President. God gave us an explicit command, not a suggestion, mind you, a command not to speak abusively of our rulers. Why? Well, in the case of our political rulers, the chances of them hearing you are very slim. Not too many of us will call our public officials; we just talk about them behind their backs. So if the possibility of being heard is heavily lacking, why should we watch what we say about them? Because words have power. Proverbs 18:21 tells us that death and life are in the power of the tongue.

You may think this is farfetched but it actually happened. Some one I know had a tiny dog that I literally hated. Every time I got around that dog it was acting like a gangster. All it needed to resemble one was a pin-striped suit and a cigar. And it had the nastiest disposition I've ever seen. So being the caring person that I am, whenever I got near the dog, I would whisper in its ear, "Why don't you go somewhere and die?" I had heard sermons on speaking and the tongue but wasn't sure if I fully understood or believed it at that time. (And no, me telling the dog to die was not an experiment.)

One day, the owner called crying. When I asked her what was wrong, she sobbed, "My dog is dead."

"What happened?" I asked, secretly thinking, "All right."

"I don't know," she replied. "He was in the front yard and just started running across the street. He didn't even slow down to wait on the cars. It's as though he was deaf and blind."

I felt like a heel. I don't know if she knew how I felt about her dog or not, but she was heart broken and through her tears I learned how this dog had been her companion for a long time. She lived alone and he had brought her much happiness. But that incident really proved to me our words have power. I still feel like I convinced the dog to die.

God's Word is full of instructions concerning the use of the tongue. Proverbs 6:16,17 tells us God hates a lying tongue, a false witness and someone that sows discord among the brethren. What instrument do we use to accomplish all that? The tongue.

James 3:6 tells us our tongue defiles the whole body. What you say is what you get and the tongue brings on most of our trouble. Don't constantly blame the devil for *your* lack of controlling your tongue. Instead of looking before we leap, shouldn't we think before we speak?

Chapter three of the book of James is one of the most potent chapters in the Bible. If followed, it will help the Body in showing the fruit of the Spirit. Verses eight through eleven goes on to tell us it is humanly impossible to control the tongue. We bless God with it and curse men with it. Out of our mouths comes blessings and cursing. We're double minded.

The Indians used to have a saying. "White man speak with forked tongue.' What comes to your mind when you hear of a forked tongue? A reptile. A snake. The same creature that lent itself to Satan in the Garden. Are you lending yourself to a snake?

Proverbs 13:3 says, "He that keepeth his mouth keepeth his life. But he that openeth wide his lips shall have destruction." In other words, shut your mouth and live or run it and die.

Finally, let me show you something God showed me some time back. It is awesome.

In the book of Luke we have two accounts of impending births. Both of these births would change the world and man would never be the same. God spoke both into existence; an angel delivered news of the conception of both. Both mothers-to-be were in a position where pregnancy was not a likelihood.

Elizabeth, the cousin of Mary, Jesus' mother, was married to a priest named Zacharias. They were both righteous before God, and tried diligently to obey all the commandments and ordinances. They had no child because Elizabeth was barren and at this particular time, they were both well on in years. So the likelihood of conception was almost impossible to expect.

Zacharias' duty in the temple was to burn incense and on this particular day, the multitude of the people was praying outside the temple while he was inside burning incense. While he was performing his duties an angel appeared to him and stood on the right side of the altar. When Zacharias saw him, it scared him pretty badly.

But the angel calmed him and began to explain his mission. He explained that his prayer had been heard and his wife Elizabeth would bear a son and he was to call his name John. Now it is very obvious that if he was told his prayer was to be answered, then it stands to reason he must have prayed for a son.

The angel went on to tell him how great his son would be in the sight of the Lord and how righteous the son would be…that the Lord would go before him in the spirit and power of Elijah.

Then Zacharias asked the angel, "Whereby shall I know this? For I am well stricken in years."

Now can you believe this guy? Here was an old man, who played a major part in the work of the ministry, ministered to God's people which means he probably had several occasions to tell them to have faith in the Lord, asks God for a son, came face to face with an angel who told him his prayer was answered, and this guy had the nerve to say, "Whereby shall I know this?" In other words, how will I know you're telling me the truth? Give me proof. And the angel did. I think it was a little more than he bargained for, but nonetheless, the angel gave him proof.

What kind of proof? He shut him up! For the duration of the pregnancy he shut him up. The dude wasn't allowed to speak. And the reason the proof was so harsh was because good 'ole Zach didn't believe the angel's words. It says so right in Luke 1:20. The guy prayed for a son, who, at that age, would have been a miracle to say the least, and then doubted God was answering the prayer. The Bible says we are justified or condemned by *our* words and I believe God couldn't take the chance of 'ole Zach coming out of the temple and saying, "Hey folks. Guess what just happened. An angel appeared to me right there in the temple and said Elizabeth and I would be having a son. Now I believe in angels but considering our age, I will have to see it to believe it."

Had he spoken those words, he could have probably had enough power in them to abort the mission. There is power in our words. Now let's see what Mary said when the angel appeared to her. And keep in mind, she too, was in a position where the likelihood of giving birth at that time was somewhat unbelievable.

Mary, a young virgin, engaged to Joseph, a wedding in the future. A very righteous woman, one who obeyed the Lord. I like to think that Mary was somewhat shy and timid. Maybe she was home minding her own business or looking through a monthly edition of Bride's magazine. Maybe she was sitting at her mirror trying to decide how to wear her hair at the wedding or considering a lovely pattern for silverware. At any rate, the last thing she had on her mind was an angel popping in unannounced.

The angel gave her a greeting saying, "Hail, thou that are highly favored, the Lord is with thee: blessed art thou among women." (Luke 1:28)

Now notice here Mary didn't jump up and scream, she didn't dial 911 or even yell for her father. The only thing on her mind was what he had said, and *that* is what she was troubled over, wondering what kind of a greeting this was. (Verse 29) She was probably thinking, "Who, me? Blessed among women? I'm just a common woman about to be married. I'm nothing special that the Lord would send an angel to greet me." But the angel calmed her by telling her she had found favor with God. Then he announced his mission.

She was going to have a child. She hadn't asked for one at that time, or at least, if she had, she would have asked the Lord to bless her womb *after* the wedding. After all, there's nothing wrong with asking God for children, as long as you wait until you're married to try to get them.

She was going to be a mommy and the conception would be *before* she got married. She could have felt a little uneasy. But she didn't. She didn't even doubt his words. She could have said, "Look man, I'm not married yet and we live in a society where good girls just don't do stuff like that and no, not me. Go find somebody else." But she didn't.

Instead, she humbly accepted what God had said and her only question was, "Can you tell me how this will happen since I'm a virgin and have never known a man? I do not doubt you in the least, if this is what God wants, then no problem. I've never known a man and don't intend to until I'm married. So just out of curiosity, how?"

I really like what she said after the angel gladly explained it to her. I can see him now. He knew her reputation was at stake. He knew her fiancée would probably hit the roof and he knew she was probably scared. I like to think at that time he might have smiled at her a little, and in a voice so tender it was almost a whisper. "The Holy Ghost shall come upon thee, and the power of the Highest shall overshadow thee: therefore also that holy thing which shall be born of thee shall be called the Son of God."

And Mary didn't strut her stuff. She didn't go and tell everybody God loved her more than anyone else. She just very humbly accepted what was before her and said, "Behold the handmaid of the Lord: be it unto me according to thy word." (Verse 38)

Two births. Two women who shouldn't have had children at that time. And both announcements were accepted in different ways. Their words sealed the deal. Their words had destiny. Their words had power. Jesus is the Head and we, the Body, need to let Him do the speaking.

9

I Get the Sensation Of...

On the top of your brain and slightly to the left is the sensory cortex. This controls three body functions that are very important to us.

Bodily sensation. Touch, taste, smell. We take them for granted so much. The Bible says to give God thanks in all things. But no one seems to do anything but complain when we have a cold and our taste buds go on vacation. After all, the tongue is there for other reasons than to commit spiritual murder.

It's a home...a home for taste buds, and we should take care of it. For instance, sweep it every day with a toothbrush or help stop air pollution and use a mouthwash. Install a fire alarm by cooling you coffee before drinking it. Take care of your tongue.

Without our taste buds intact we'd be deprived of a lot of things that make our life delightful. Like gagging when we've tasted a bad medicine, or eating your mother-in-law's cooking, or having a Kodak moment when you're watching your children taste lemon juice for the first time. And where would we be if we could not exercise our intellectual achievements by occasionally sticking out our tongue at someone we don't like? Hey...the tongue is a very useful weapon.

It also has a complex system of muscles that makes it possible to move food around as you chew (this comes in handy when you're chewing someone out) and then forming the food into a ball for easy swallowing. Taste buds are able to distinguish between four major types of flavor: sweet, sour, salt and bitter. Mine usually notice pungent flavors like goat cheese.

Speaking of flavors, have you ever noticed how a dog gulps its food? It never actually chews; it just swallows once the food is positioned. My dog (whom I secretly think is a horse in disguise) never sniffs anything or takes time to sample. She just inhales. I wonder if dogs have taste buds. Oh, well, moving on...

There are other things we can taste besides food and medicine, other things that are really not physically digestible. For instance, Job could discern the taste between good and perverse things in Job 6:30. Even David liked to savor every tidbit of God's Word in his mouth. (Psalms 119:103) How many Christians today will read the Word then sit back and continue to roll it around in the mouth just to let it linger on the palate, wanting the flavor to last and last like the chewing gum commercials. What if your taste buds suddenly went into a coma? You wouldn't be able to taste any thing.

Once one of my cousins came to visit. He lived next door and he hadn't been over in a few days to play. When he came in, my mother welcomed him and he told us he had had a very bad cold. (Which reminds me…how can a person have a *good* cold?) Mom offered to fix him something to eat and as he bit into the food he said, "Boy, that's good. That's the first food I've been able to taste all week.' His taste buds had been in a coma. Can you imagine living like that all your life, not being able to taste anything? Boring!!!

Jesus spoke of Himself as being the food quite often. The last supper is one incident wherein He did this. John 6 gives a beautiful account of how He refers to Himself as Bread…Living Bread. But there is an even more awesome account of Living Bread in the Old Testament. If you've ever studied typology, you would almost loose your Pharisaic dignity and shout when you read it. Go get your Bible again and turn to Exodus 16:14.

The first thing to notice is the time the manna fell. The children gathered it after the dew had gone up, meaning it had fallen through the night. Jesus was born at night, (Luke 2:8-11) because He was the Light of the world. Numbers 11:9 tells us that after the dew had fallen, the manna fell on the dew. It never touched the ground. It was clean. Jesus was sinless.

This 'small thing' mentioned here in verse 14 is a perfect picture of Christ's humility. The shape of it, round, signifies His eternal being, Everlasting, the Alpha and Omega, from beginning to end. Verse 15 shows where it came from. "This is the Bread which the Lord hath given you to eat." Manna from Heaven.

Verse 16-20 is joyous in that God commanded the children to gather according to their eating, an omer for every person in the family. An omer is a lot of food, equaling about six and three fourths pints. And it says the children gathered…some more, some less. But they were told not to take more than they could eat. If they did it turned bad. I'd say breeding worms and stinking would be bad, wouldn't you?

Now compare John 6:63 with John 6:41, 42, and 52. You will see that Christ will give Himself without restraint, but we have no more of Him than our faith will appropriate. Joshua 1:3 says God told Joshua that every place the sole of his foot walked on would be given unto him. This is our title to possession. We can have all the Manna we want and it tastes *soooo* good. (Exodus 16:21) All we have to do is walk to it and eat. Do as we are instructed in Psalms 34.8. "O, taste, and see that the Lord is good."

Last of all in verse 18 it says, "...he that gathered much had nothing over, and he that gathered little had no lack..." Jesus, the Manna from Heaven, satisfies. In considering Jesus as being Manna and Jesus being the Bread of Life I like to remember Proverbs 30:8. "Feed me with food convenient for me."

This verse falls right into line with Matthew 6:9-13. Jesus was teaching the disciples how to pray and part of those instructions were in verse 11 where He says, "Give us this day our daily bread." Now compare that verse with the one just quoted in Proverbs 30:8. Then compare both of them with the scriptures in Exodus 16:18 where we learned that they always had the right amount. Jesus satisfies!!

The Shemoneh Esreh, or the Eighteen Blessings, is a group of Hebrew Prayers. Shemoneh Esreh means eighteen, which is calculated eight plus ten. The number eight, in the numerology of God, stands for the new beginning and the number ten stands for the Law. This in itself is beautiful. But there is something more tasteful about the whole thing.

Verse 11 of how Jesus taught the disciples to pray in which it says, "Give us this day our daily bread" actually is asking God to give us just what we need, no more, no less. Likewise, the scripture in Proverbs 30:8. But the awesome thing is these verses line up with one of the Shemoneh Esreh Blessings that are recited by the Jews as they worship. That blessing is number nine and it says, "Bless this year for us, O Lord our God, and all its varied produce, that it be for good; provide dew and rain as a blessing on the face of the earth, satisfy us with The goodness, and bless this year like the good years. Blessed art Thou Lord, who blesses the years."

In comparing the Eighteen Blessings with the instructions of how to pray as Jesus demonstrated in Matthew 6 we can see something quite remarkable. "Give us this day our daily bread," is a request for our needs to be satisfied. Jesus appeals to our sense of taste and He satisfies. And this verse not only parallels with Proverbs 30:8 and Exodus 16:18 but it parallels with numbers seven, eight, nine, and ten of the Semoneh Esreh. These four prayers or blessings are:

Number 7: Look upon us in our suffering, and fight our struggles, redeem us speedily, for Thy name's sake, for Thou are a mighty Redeemer. Blessed are thou, Lord, Redeemer of Israel.

Number 8: Heal us, O Lord, and we shall be healed, save us and we shall be saved, for Thou art our glory. Send complete healing for our every illness, for

Thou, divine King, art the faithful, merciful Physician. Blessed art Thou, Lord, who heals the sick of His people, Israel.

Number 9: Quoted above.

Number 10: Sound the great shofar to proclaim our freedom, lift up a banner for the ingathering of our exiles, and bring us together from the four corners of the earth. Blessed art Thou, Lord, who gathers together the dispersed of His people Israel.

"O, taste, and see that the Lord is good." (Psalms 34:8) The Manna was good to the taste. Jesus is the Manna. Bread is good to the taste. Jesus is the Bread of Life. "Give us this day our daily bread." The Jews pray the Eighteen Blessings and four of those line up with the above Scriptures. "Marvelous Are Thy Works" (Psalms 139:14 Capitalization added) This sort of thing makes me ever so glad that my ability to taste is with the tongue, and the tongue of the Body is in the Head.

◆   ◆   ◆

When our boys were little, the eldest like to play jokes on the younger one. I remember one time in particular when Tony, the eldest, was around six or seven. His brother whom we called Jody at the time (he's grown now and prefers to be called Joe) always called him 'Brudder' because he had a hard time pronouncing the word brother. Joe was about two or three at the time.

Anyway, their dad told Tony to go into the bathroom of our bedroom and hide under the sink in the cabinet. Gene was then going to tell Jody that he was going to flush Tony down the commode. Tony ran to hide and Gene told his *little white lie* and then flushed the commode. As soon as Tony heard the commode flush, he yelled out, "Good-bye, Jodyyyyy."

Poor little Joe ran up and down the hall to each bathroom and stuck his head right over the commode yelling, "Come back, Brudder, come back!"

Being the mother I was, I told Gene that was a cruel joke, but I couldn't help laughing. Joe was so funny running up and down the hall. But after they had played so many jokes on him through the years, he finally wised up. Now when Tony calls and says, "Hey, Man, I got something to tell you that's real serious," Joe always replies with, "Yeah, right! I smell a rat."

Another sensation is smell.

Once there was a man that was constantly complaining about the bad smell. Everywhere he went he complained about the stench. People he worked with and the people he went to church with always dreaded to see him come. Finally, someone got the courage to tell him he had Limburger cheese in his mustache. Sometimes I think Christians are like that, always complaining about the smell, not knowing they are carrying the stench around with them.

One of my daughters-in-law has a green thumb. I told her it was just molded but she didn't believe me. Some people have no sense of humor. Anyway, because of this my house smells like roses quite often during the season and I have an ample supply of rose tea. It is so nice to come in and take a deep breath. So nice to just stand by the bar and breathe. She even sends me roses. Eat your heart out all you other mothers-in-law. This one is taken. She has me spoiled.

Roses and rose petals are semi-secret demonstrations of the love she and our son share. It's beautiful to watch her expressions when something happens between them and roses are included. Her eyes sparkle and she looks radiant. Of course, I just don't have the heart to tell her that she doesn't know him as well as I do.

Every time I see this unspoken exchange of love between them I think of the Rose of Sharon. So many times in the Song of Solomon comparisons are made to a sweet fragrance. Both the groom and the bride are forever giving each other compliments. It's a constant tender comparison to the precious oils of that day. There fragrances were priceless and so was the love portrayed in Solomon. Our love with the Rose of Sharon should be just as priceless and smell just as fragrant.

Incense: According to Webster, it is a material used to produce a fragrant odor when burned. A pleasing scent.

Exodus 30:34-38 gives a detailed account of how to make incense and why it was used. Verse 38 will kinda scare you a little if you stop and think of all the different fragrances we have on the market today. It tells you explicitly what would happen to the people if they made the fragrance just to sniff because it smelled good. Why all this strictness about a fragrance? It shouldn't seem to make that much difference to God about an odor since He created the nose and odors to begin with, but…

Go get your Bible again. (And this time don't put it back because you may need it again.) Turn to Psalms 141:2. David is figuratively using his prayer as an incense. It reads, "Let my prayer be set forth before thee as incense: and the lifting up of my hands as the evening sacrifice." He wants God to find his request a delightful odor. And what about Malachi 1:11?

It says, "For from the rising of the sun even unto the going down of the same my name shall be great among the Gentiles; and in every place incense shall be offered unto my name, and a pure offering; for my name shall be great among the heathen, saith the Lord of hosts" This prophecy has, and still is, coming to pass.

His name is great among the Gentiles and incense is offered to Him…the incense of prayer.

Daily His nostrils breathe deeply when His children come to communicate with Him. And we have this abused liberty because of another sweet smelling savor listed in Ephesians 5:2. "And walk in love, as Christ also hath loved us, and hath given himself for us an offering and a sacrifice to God for a sweet smelling savor."

The offering and sacrifice of Christ to God was accepted because of its purity and unconditional love.

I guess the greatest part about smell and odors is how it is depicted in Revelations. (Did you put your Bible back? Go get it.) Turn to Revelations 5:8.

Did you know God puts your prayers in a bowl, a golden vial? And why are the twenty-four elders holding them? This has to do with another representation that will be discussed in a later chapter. Now turn to Revelations 8:3,4 and read what happens to the sweet smelling bowl full of prayers.

Have you ever talked to someone and all they say is that their prayers don't even seem to reach the ceiling? Now it stands to reason, if He keeps filling the bowl, the bowl would eventually get filled up and run over so He has to do something with them. He has to be answering them because He's certainly not putting them in storage.

I can't help but believe that in this particular incident God is showing us how important our prayers are. We know they smell good to Him and like most fragrances, they have a lingering effect. Could it be that God answers our prayers and we don't want to accept the answer?

And could the prayers in Revelations 8:3,4 be the lingering effect of the incense of prayers and God wants to savor every moment because He's getting ready to do something really outstanding? After all, right before this happens there is silence in Heaven for a while.

It reminds me of what it is like at a circus when the trapeze artists are doing something spectacular. The audience stands, their gaze captivated, the silence is deafening. Then as the artist swings back and forth gaining momentum, with the audience wondering how long it will take, he suddenly lets go of the swing, and hurling himself into the air, he somersaults three times.

Just as the crowd is ready to pronounce him dead, he grabs hold of his partner. Where there previously was total silence in the arena, the crowd now roars because he has performed a remarkable feat. Hang in there on the sweet smell of prayer and you will see God perform a remarkable feat for you, too. Let me share something with you about prayer that I just recently read. My daughter-in-law, Lisa, received this through email and sent it to me.

The Smell of Rain

A cold March wind danced around the dead of night in Dallas as the doctor walked into the small hospital room of Diana Blessing. Still groggy from surgery, her husband David held her hand as they braced themselves for the latest news. That afternoon of March 10, 1989, complications had forced Diana, only twenty-four weeks pregnant, to undergo an emergency cesarean to deliver the couple's new daughter, Danae Lu Blessing. At twelve inches and weighing only one pound and nine ounces, they already knew she was perilously premature. Still the doctor's soft words dropped like bombs.

"I don't think she's going to make it," he said as kindly as he could. "There's only a 10% chance she will live through the night, and even then, if by some slim chance she does make it, her future could be a very cruel one."

Numb with disbelief, David and Diana listened as the doctor described the devastating problems Danae would likely face if she survived. She would never walk, she would never talk, she would probably be blind, and she would certainly be prone to other catastrophic conditions from cerebral palsy to complete mental retardation, and on and on. "No! No!" was all Diana could say.

She and David, with their five-year-old son Dustin, had long dreamed of the day they would have a daughter to become a family of four. Now, within a matter of hours, that dream was slipping away.

Through the dark hours of morning as Danae held onto life by the thinnest thread, Diana slipped in and out of sleep, growing more and more determined that their tiny daughter would live…and live to be a healthy, happy young girl. But David, fully awake and listening to additional dire details of their daughter's chances of ever leaving the hospital alive, much less healthy, knew he must confront his wife with the inevitable. David walked in and said that they needed to talk about making funeral arrangements.

Diana remembers, "I felt so bad for him because he was doing everything, trying to include me in what was going on, but I just wouldn't listen. I couldn't listen. I said, "No, that is not going to happen, no way! I don't care what the doctors say: Danae is not going to die! One day she will be just fine, and she will be coming home with us!" As if willed to live by Diana's determination, Danae clung to life with the help of every medical machine and marvel her miniature body could endure. But as those first days passed, a new agony set in for David and Diana.

Because Danae's under developed nervous system was essentially raw, the lightest kiss or caress only intensified her discomfort, and so they couldn't even cradle their tiny baby girl against their chests to offer the strength of their love. All they could do as Danae struggled alone beneath the ultraviolet light in the tangle of tubes and wires was to pray that God would stay close to their precious little girl.

There was never a moment when Danae suddenly grew stronger. But as the weeks went by, she did slowly gain an ounce of weight here and an ounce of strength there. At last, when Danae turned two months old, her parents were able to hold her in their arms for the very first time. And two months later, though doctors continued to gently but grimly warn that her chances of surviving, much less living any kind of normal life, were next to zero.

Danae went home from the hospital just as her mother had predicted. Today, five years later, Danae is a petite but feisty young girl with glittering gray eyes and an unquenchable zest for life. She shows no signs, whatsoever, of any mental or physical impairment. Simply put, she is everything a little girl can be and more. But that happy ending is far from the end of this story.

One blistering afternoon in the summer of 1996, near her home, Danae was sitting in her mother's lap in the bleachers of a local ballpark where her brother Dustin's baseball team was practicing. As always, Danae was chattering non-stop with her mother and several other adults sitting nearby when she suddenly fell silent. Hugging her arms across her chest, Danae asked, "Do you smell that?"

Her mother replied, "Yes, I think we're about to get wet; it smells like rain. Still caught in the moment, Danae shook her head, patted her thin shoulders with her small hands and loudly announced, "No, it smells like Him. It smells like God when you lay your head on His chest."

Tears blurred Diana's eyes as Danae then happily hopped down to play with the other children. Before the rains came, her daughter's words confirmed what Diana and all the members of the extended Blessing family had known, at least in their hearts, all along. During those long days and nights of her first two months of life, when her nerves were too sensitive for them to touch her, God was holding Danae on His chest and it is His loving scent that she remembered so well.

We in the Body most times find it hard to take a deep breath and inhale the fragrance of God. Jesus, our Head, breathed deeply quite often during the day, when He would steal away and pray. Why not take a walk to your bedroom and get a good, deep breath of fresh air.... for the sake of the Body.

◆   ◆   ◆

The last bodily sensation is touch.

Touch is a very important part of our lives. It can be pleasant, like when mommy kisses a child that has just fallen and gotten a booboo, or it can be scary, like when you turn down the thermostat and it suddenly plunges to forty degrees outside and your 200 pound dog decides it's to cold to stay where she is, and jumps right in the middle of your stomach while you're asleep. (Dumb dog, She's a horse in disguise, I tell you.)

Touch tells you when it hurts and when it feels good. One thing about touch that really cracks me up is when they show people on television that are in a romantic moment. The man gently places his hand on the side of the woman's head and staring lovingly into her eyes, he slowly runs his hand through her hair. What I don't understand about all this is it always seems to have some positive effect. What is it about touching the hair? It's as though he can't pucker until he feels the hair. Puckering and hair have nothing in common.

There are two types of touching. One is physical and one is emotional. Physically the touch can be nice or painful. For instance, one day, Amber, one of our granddaughters, smacked her elbow on the door. The impact sent a tingly feeling down her arm so I said, "You must have struck your funny bone.' It seemed like the logical remark at the time.

But Amber, still smarting from the bump, said, "Funny bone? It hurts, Nanny! Do you see me laughing?" Whoever thought of calling it a funny bone, anyway?

Then, of course, the emotional touch. This touch will bring all kinds of reactions. There's the touch of when your daughter-in-law has a problem and she wants to talk. Tears begin to run down her cheeks and she says, "Nanny, what's wrong with me? Why am I feeling this way? So defeated, so alone."

The touch in your heart makes you want to reach out and hold her. But the wisdom God has given you through the years makes you say, "Baby, all you need is to go into the bedroom and talk to Daddy. There are times when He wants to hold you in His arms and just rock you to sleep. You're Father's little girl and He knows what you need. A little TLC always works wonders."

Two or three hours later, she reappears with a smile on her face and informs me that *Daddy* wasn't in a talking mood. All He did was hold her and let her cry. Then He kissed her cheek and said, "Feel better?"

No reason for the tears, just a longing to be *'Daddy's little girl.'* There was a song written a few years ago entitled *'Daddy's Hands'.* It was a country and western song, but it sure is true with my Heavenly Father.

There's another touch of emotion that is so satisfying it is beyond words. And that's when your other daughter-in-law calls from work and says, "Nanny, may we come down tonight and you teach us from the Bible?"

"Of course!! I'll even throw in dinner."

I guess you've figured out by now that I love my two daughters-in-law. They're more like my daughters. They can disagree with me and indeed; there have been times when they've even changed my mind. We don't always see eye to eye, like when Lisa goes on a diet.

This kid is as skinny as a rail. She's so skinny she could drink a cherry soda and pass for a thermometer. If she turned sideways and stuck out her tongue she would pass for a zipper. I think there should be a law against people being so little. You'd never know by looking at her that she has given birth. It's disgusting. And she's the only one I know that can fit a 28-hour day into 16 and still come out with every hair in place. Besides this, she looks so cute when she's wearing her baseball hat.

Then there's the time when I'm sort of caught up on concentration and not very talkative and Diane will say, "Nanny, are you upset with me? You're not saying very much. Have I done something wrong?"

This girl doesn't have a wrong bone in her body. She prays too much for that to happen. She's the first to say, "I'm sorry" when there is an argument. The first to apologize when she's too sick to get out of bed and she thinks she's put you to any trouble. Her eyes sparkle when she laughs (which is quite often) and gathers tears when someone gets saved, (which she says in not nearly enough).

Our boys are always pulling something on somebody and at times when we're all together, we laugh so hard it hurts. We literally took God at His word when He said, "A merry heart doeth good like a medicine." (Proverbs 17:22)

You see all of this is touching. It touches the heart when your children know they can talk to you. It touches the heart when you can stand back and see a living God in the homes of your children and their families. Don't get me wrong. We have our problems, but we also have the Problem Solver. And this…is touching.

Then there's the physical. Did you know that Jesus was a doctor's and mortician's greatest nightmare? Everywhere He went, He was always touching someone and healing them or touching someone and they rose from the dead. He would put a funeral home out of business in a hurry. Of course, there was a time when He wouldn't let anyone touch Him. (John 20:17)

I often wondered, during my early stage of Christian development, why He did that. One day God showed me and I saw how simple it was. You see, God had already told Moses that the priests should not touch anything unclean before entering the tabernacle. As a matter of fact, once Aaron was consecrated he was not supposed to touch anything unclean at all. Exodus, Numbers and Leviticus carry passages concerning how the priest is supposed to be clean and in touching anything dead, that cleanliness would be defiled.

The Bible tells us in Colossians 2:13 that we are dead in our sins. At the time she saw Him, the blood hadn't been offered, just shed. So Mary would have been basically unclean at the time she saw Christ outside the tomb. The Bible also tells us in Hebrews 4:14 that Jesus is our High Priest.

"But He told Thomas to thrust his hand into His side," you may argue.

True. But only after the High Priest entered the Holy of Holies and presented the sacrificial blood for the atoning of their sins and came out of the tabernacle, did he allow anyone to touch Him. I believe that sometimes between the time Mary saw Jesus outside the tomb and the time He told Thomas to touch His side, the Lord of Lords ascended to Heaven and entered the Holy of Holies and presented His cleansing blood as a sacrifice for our sins. After God accepted the sacrificial blood, Christ then came out and later Thomas was told to touch Him. God cannot go against His own words and if Mary had touched Christ outside the tomb, He would not have been clean and His blood would not have been accepted.

Touching involves a decision. We can touch the unclean things of the world or we can touch Christ. How do we touch Him?

We can touch His garment and be healed. We can touch His heart with true repentance and be saved. We can touch His compassion when we cry. We can touch His nail-scarred hands when we are stumbling and He will hold us up. We can touch Him with our faith and see the mountains move. Most of all, we can touch Him by kneeling at the foot of the cross and proclaiming Him Lord and King. And one day praise the Lord, we will touch Him physically.

Our sensations are important. It's what puts the spice into life. Each sensation can be dealt with physically or emotionally. But the Body is not capable of experiencing these sensations to the fullest yet. Paul said in I Corinthians 13:11-12, "When I was a child, I spake as a child, I understood as a child, I thought as a child; but when I became a man, I put away childish things. For now we see through a glass darkly: but then face to face; now I know in part: but then shall I know even as also I am known."

One day the curse will be lifted from this world. Cantaloupe will taste sweeter, roses will smell stronger, and the touch of His hand as He wipes the tears from the eyes of the Body, will be a gentle caress.

10

Grandma, What Big Ears You Have

The hearing center is also controlled by the cerebral hemisphere. The center is located on the left side of the brain.

Children have a remarkable way of saying whatever is on their minds. One sure way to tell if the members of a church have been having roast pastor for dinner is by the way the children behave and speak. If nice things are being said the children will flock around him. But let him preach on something that goes against the grain and the members go home mad, rest assured before to many days have past, the pastor will notice a difference.

Why are we so quick to listen to negative speaking? I often wondered why the real *spiritual* people think gossip is the worst thing in a church. The gossips are quickly labeled and sometimes ostracized.

But why is it that the ones who *listen* to the garbage are never labeled or pushed aside after they let it grow within them? For instance:

Once there was a woman that appeared to be very spiritual. She was always speaking of the great services they had at church and how God was dealing with the people. I had the opportunity to speak with her on several occasions but always at a festive affair. Her attitude was usually one of excitement and enthusiasm. So based on this, naturally, when she (whom I began to affectionately and secretly call Sister Shoutite) called my office for an appointment, I was somewhat surprised.

"This woman has a grip on life. What could she possibly need counseling for?" were my first thoughts.

Week after week I would watch Sister Shoutite come through the door, shoulders sagging, breathe a deep sigh, and fall into the chair. Eyes on the floor and in a quivering voice she would whisper, "Hello."

"And how are you today?" I'd smile and ask.

"Oh, okay I guess."

The first time that happened I responded with, "My, my. You sound sort of down. What could have happened to cause such a heaviness?"

"Well, yesterday at church, we were having such a good time. The Spirit was moving freely and the pastor was preaching so hard. The things he said were really touching me and I began to cry. I can't help it. I'm just an emotional person. Anyway, after the service, I happened to pass by some ladies that were standing in a group talking. They did not know I was there and I over heard the church gossip make some remarks about me and how emotional I am. She said she thought I was just putting on a show because nobody could cry as easily or as often as I do. That really hurt my feelings."

Every week it was the same. Every week she would have a sad story to tell or relate some words that had filtered back to her that originally began with the same person. She was always repeating how emotional she was, able to cry or shout at just about anything pertaining to God, and then this other lady, (whom I secretly began to refer to as Sister Blabite) would always have a remark to make that would burst her bubble. After a few weeks of this, I began to dread her coming. Nothing I gave her from Scripture seemed to help. When her time was up, I was as depressed as she was. And to make matters worse, I was beginning to agree with her about why didn't the pastor do something about the gossip and reprimand her? How could this preacher let this go on and on? Didn't he realize Sister Blabite was causing great turmoil in Sister Shoutite's life? I decided to grab hold of the horns of the altar and not let go until God gave me an answer on how to help this lady. That night I hit my knees.

"Father, please help me. I don't know what to do to help her. She is overcome by the remarks this gossip, Sister Blabite, is casting her way. After all these weeks, I've watched a vibrant woman sag beneath the load and now she finds it hard to cry or shout or praise You in any way. Her joy has been stolen and we both know how You feel about gossips. I need an answer and I need it quickly. I just don't know if I want to hear any more of it."

"Then why do you listen to it?" came the reply.

"What? It's my job, Lord. I'm a counselor. That's what I do. I listen, and then offer Scripture as to how to handle the problem."

"Fine. Then offer her Scripture. She can only defeat Satan with My Word. But you must offer her the weapon. Tell her that not only did I caution my children about gossiping, I cautioned them about *listening*."

Now that one stumped me. So wondering what He was talking about I immediately started searching the Word. I looked up every Scripture I could find on ears, speaking and listening. And do you know what I found?

I was shocked! I'd heard so many sermons on gossips, speaking bad things into existence, and how to watch your mouth. But some where along the line, some of these preachers had missed something of great importance. Speaking involves making a sound. *Listening* involves a response to that sound. So when I read what the Lord had to say about it, I had my answer. At the next appointed time I was armed and ready.

The door opened and Sister Shoutite walked in.

"Hello," came the familiar defeated whisper.

"Come in, come in. Have a seat and let's began. I just know God is going to do great things today."

"I suppose," she sighed.

"I don't suppose. I know."

She looked up at me and sort of seemed surprised that I had that much confidence but I encouraged her to tell me about her week.

"Well, it started out all right. I finally got over her last vindictive remarks and gossip and determined I was going to tell the preacher that if he didn't stop her I was going to leave the church. So I made an appointment with him and told him how I felt."

"And his reply?" I asked.

"Well, he agreed with me that her gossip was a problem. And he promised he would talk to her. But before he had a chance, she did it again. I'll be glad when he does and she is either put in her place or removed from the church. I haven't been able to do my own tasks or help in the church because of her gossip and I stay depressed all the time."

"So why do you listen to it?"

She gasped. "Well, what do you mean by that?"

"Exactly what I said. It's like deliberately drinking poison. If you know it's going to kill you, why do you keep drinking it? Her poison is sucking the life right out of you and yet, you keep going back for more."

"But God says somewhere in the Bible that people are not to be talebearers."

"Yes, He does. But have you read what He says to those of us that listen? Take the Bible on the table beside you. Open it to Mark 4:24. Read it aloud."

Turning the pages to the suggested text, Sister Shoutite reluctantly found the passage and began to read aloud.

"And he said unto them, Take heed what ye hear; with what measure ye mete, it shall be measured to you: and unto you that hear shall more be given."

"What did it say again?" I encouraged her.

"Well, whatever measure we deal out will be measured back to us and those that hear shall be given more."

"Do you see what He is telling you? He is saying to consider carefully what you hear. And I believe with all my heart He is telling us to discard anything that is not praising and lifting up the name of the Lord. Did you hear me? Discard it. Get rid of it. Throw it away. It's not useable; it's destructive, so why hang on to it? If you change churches, I feel you will be acting out of God's will because He is not the author of confusion. He tells us to go to our brethren and try to straighten out the problem, for the sake of unity. If you run, you are acting against God's instructions because He is not capable of being double minded and He will not tell you to change churches and tell the rest of the world to go to their brethren. He cannot, and will not, go against His own Word.

So you have a choice. You can confront her and do it God's way or you can run. Either way, take heed what you hear, because this is destroying you. And if you choose to run, then we will no longer be able to come together to solve this problem because the problem will always be there, and frankly, I don't think I should hear it any more. I'm going to *take heed what I hear, also.*"

Of course, she was a little upset. Actually, she was a lot upset because by this time she had developed a certain satisfaction of being the center of pity. But I stood my ground and she stop coming. My depression left and I felt like a weight had been lifted. I no longer dreaded seeing my clients come through the door. I had taken heed to what I was hearing and considered it carefully before either applying it or discarding it.

It was almost a year before I saw her again. During this time she had kept harboring tense feelings toward me and changed churches. Within a few weeks the monster had surfaced again. People were gossiping about her once more. After a few painful episodes of this, she remembered my words. But instead of confronting the one that was guilty that time, she courageously attended her old church, which was where her heart was anyway. After much prayer, confrontation and spiritual warfare she gained the victory. No, the gossip didn't stop and the preacher didn't rebuke. Sister Shoutite was the one to change. She was the one to start obeying the Word and after she started taking heed to what she heard, her life began to flourish.

Everyone knows, if they will admit it or not, that what we hear influences the way we feel. There have been times I've met someone and liked the first impression. Then someone comes along and says something like, "You better be careful around that person. You just don't know what they're really like."

And if I'm not careful, the next time I see them, I'll be so on guard they can feel the tension radiating from me and not even know what's going on. There's a good way to discourage gossip. The next time someone says to you, "Do you know what so and so did to me?" just look at them and say, "No, and I don't want to."

I get a kick out of pestering our grandchildren. For instance, Callie will believe anything I tell her. If she hears it from Nanny, she *knows* it's true. A good example of this happened just recently.

We had all gone out to eat seafood and as the hostess was leading us to our table I turned to Callie and said, "Too bad, baby, it's Thursday."

"Why Nanny?" she asked.

"Well, this restaurant doesn't feed little girls on Thursdays, just Fridays. I'll fix you something when we get home. OK?"

She turned green but she sure looked relieved when the waitress took her order.

The point is people who trust you will listen to anything. And it is scary to think of some of the garbage that's been spoken to an outstretched ear. Every time someone tells my family something that's not true or insinuates they may fail at something they want to do, I get *allll* bent out of shape, especially if it relates to something from the Bible.

Not long ago someone I love very deeply was regularly calling me and asking me to pray for her. The reason was she constantly felt defeated. It seemed that every time she went to church she came out feeling worse than when she went in.

The preacher, although I'm sure he meant well, was always preaching on lazy Christians. It got to the point if she was not in church five days out of seven, she was slothful. A couple of times she had worked long hours doing inventory and then she had to go home and cook, help three children with homework, do a little laundry, help the small ones with their baths and then help them say their prayers, (WHEW! I'm tired just retelling it.) she was exhausted and just fell into bed.

During the night she woke up and felt so heavy she lapsed into tears. She had not taken time to read her Bible and the guilt was eating her alive. Because of the guilt for failing God, she took on more religious activities, trying to compensate. The result was she began to feel resentment toward her pastor, and all the people that seemed to make her feel like a heel.

The next thing was a sermon on ladies wearing jewelry. Guilt again. The devil was giving her a beating and she was loosing ground fast until she began to believe the Lord was no longer pleased with her. Finally, with prayer and quoting the Scripture in Romans 8:1 where it says, "There is therefore now no condemnation to them which are in Christ Jesus, who walk not after the flesh, but after the Spirit." And in Romans 5:1 where it says, "Therefore being justified by faith, we have peace with God through our Lord Jesus Christ," she gained the victory.

Now's she's in church because she loves Him and not to keep the preacher from making little digs. Now she has total peace and when she hears legalistic remarks, she prays for those that say them.

I recently met a man that had totally given up on life. He was so defeated and had actually committed some crimes because he felt there was no need to live right. What made him feel this way? Simple.

He had at one point attended church faithfully. During these times he had carefully weighed his need for salvation. Finally, he asked for an appointment with the pastor and upon telling him he wanted to ask Christ into his heart, the pastor firmly told him he could not be saved because he had tattoos, one on each arm. This man was devastated. He acquired a great resentment toward God because he had not had any previous teachings and he felt his pastor was telling him the truth and God wasn't being fair to disqualify him for something he had done when he had no knowledge of Christ. He stopped going to church and developed a 'who cares?' attitude. When I ask him why he didn't read the Bible and find out himself, he sadly dropped his head and whispered, "I can't read or write." Then I was furious because a church is supposed to minister to the people and they should have inquired about things of this nature and started a program to teach the adults to read.

"...faith cometh by hearing..." (Romans 10:17) For anything to come by hearing you have to listen. Did you know listening to the wrong words could transfer spirits? Turn to Numbers 13 and 14. A little background here.

Moses had sent some spies into Canaan after the children of Israel had arrived at the border from the wilderness. The Bible says they searched the land from the wilderness of Zin unto Rehob, as men come to Hamath. (Numbers 13:21) These spies came back with a report saying the grapes were so big in that land they could just about stick a straw in one and start drinking Welch's. I mean they were BIG! (Slight exaggeration added)

But they also reported that the people were, too. As a matter of fact, they said the people were so big, "...we were in our own sight as grasshopper, and so we were in their sight." (Numbers 13:33) Did you know the devil sees you the same way you see yourself?

Anyway, all the spies except two, Joshua and Caleb, kept talking and the children of Israel kept *listening* until they started finding fault with God again. This provoked God so much He was ready to zap 'em. (Numbers 14:11,12)

Ever had anyone influence you that way, with negative talk? Nah, not us. We're Americans. We can't be influenced. The children were so influenced that when Joshua and Caleb tried to tell them God would see them through, they wanted to stone them. (Numbers 14:6-10)

Moses pleaded with God not to take action against them and to have mercy. Finally, God told Moses what He would do. Look at Numbers 14:20. "And the Lord said, I have pardoned according to thy word: (This means the Lord took heed to what He was hearing.) But as truly as I live, all the earth shall be filled with the glory of the Lord. Because all those men which have seen my glory, and my miracles, which I did in Egypt and in the wilderness, and have tempted me now these ten times, and have not hearkened to my voice, surely they shall not see the land which I sware unto the fathers, neither shall any of them that provoked me see it."

Now look real close at verse 24. "But my servant Caleb, because he had *another* spirit with him…" (Italics added) Another what? Spirit. Another one other than the one the rest of the spies had? Yep. So he must have had a good one and they had a bad one. How can this be when they were God's children? They didn't take heed.

God is a God of numbers. I feel the reason for this is because numbers are a universal language. No matter how many times you calculate two plus two in any language, it still equals four. The sum of any group of numbers is still the same regardless of the language. Each letter of the Hebrew alphabet has a numerical value and it is my understanding that the published works of unlocking the Bible Code is based on a numerical formula. So we easily see that numbers are important to God. Based on those thoughts let's explore a beautiful revelation here.

The word hearken is used in the Old Testament a total of two hundred thirty four times. Of those times, one hundred sixty four are used in regard to the relationship with God and man. The remaining times are used in every day walk of life situations. These one hundred sixty four are the ones we want to examine.

Forty (which is God's number for trials and tribulations) of those times, God Himself spoke the words, "But they would not hearken to my voice." (Paraphrased) But only seventeen times (God's number for victory) did man actually admit he had not hearkened.

Nine times (the number for the fruit of the Spirit) God directly tells man how he will be blessed if he will listen or hearken to His voice. However, eighteen times (the number for bondage) God warns man what will happen if he doesn't listen or hearken. Thirty six times (the number for eternal life) is man appealing to man to listen or hearken to God. And sadly enough, only sixteen times (the number for love) is man appealing to God.

Now let's break it down into percentages. We will calculate our percentages in the same manner by using the number one hundred sixty four since these scriptures deal with our relationship with God.

The first one, with forty verses of God directly saying man will not hearken to His voice is 24%. Twenty-four is the number for the priesthood. Since twenty four is priesthood and God says we will not listen, don't you think it was necessary for Christ to be the Head, or our High Priest? Now can you fully comprehend why Jesus warned us to 'take heed what we hear'?

The second was man admitting he will not listen. These seventeen scriptures are 10% (the actual percentage shows 0.103 and rounded off is .10) of the one hundred sixty four and ten is the number for the Law. God said we are created in His image and He gave us certain standards to live by, and these standards are in the Law. 24% of the time God is trying to make priests out of us, and 10% of the time man is admitting he thinks he can do it all by himself.

The third was God telling how we would be blessed if we would listen. Nine times He did this, which is 5%, and five is the number for grace. However, the next one shows God making it clear (eighteen times) what will happen if man doesn't listen and eighteen is 11% and eleven is the number for judgment.

Next we had man appealing to man to hearken to God. Twenty eight times this is recorded and it is 17% of the one hundred sixty four. Seventeen is the number of victory. Did you know that the only way to get victory over any trial or tribulation is by speaking the Word? That's how Jesus did it during the forty days He was in the wilderness and Satan tried to tempt Him. He used the Word of God. By the way, I really like what He told ole' slew foot when He said, "...Get thee hence, Satan; for it is written, Thou shalt worship the Lord THY god, and him only shalt THOU serve." (Matthew 4:10 Italics and capitalization added)

Notice the words thy and thou. Jesus wasn't just quoting a verse of scripture. He was actually *reminding* the devil of who his God is. That's *is*...not *was*. Reminding him that one of these days, he too, will bow. And the beautiful thing is, Satan took heed to what he heard. He left. Now I ask you, if Satan will take heed to what he hears when spoken from the Word, why don't we?

The sixth was God appealing to man a total of thirty six times and this is 22%. Twenty-two is God's number for Light Making Manifest. Twenty two percent of the time it is recorded that God was making His Son visible, through faith, to man. John 1:4 says it this way, "In him was life, and the life was the light of men." In the next one where man is appealing to God, it is sixteen times or 10%. We've already learned that ten stands for the Law. Once again, man thinks he can do it himself.

Is it me or does anyone else see something wrong with this picture? Does anyone else see a pattern of God constantly trying to reach out to us and us constantly refusing to hearken? Again I ask you, why doesn't man listen? Why doesn't man take heed to what we hear when it's good? The only thing the Body wants to listen to or take heed to what it hears is if it is degrading or belittling, or sowing seeds of discord among the brethren. Why don't we all just start telling those that have a loose tongue that our ears are not garbage cans? If we would quote more scripture instead of 'dear Abby' we would be a lot better off.

I'm beginning to think the fruit of the tree of knowledge of good and evil was egotism, and not an apple or a fig. Our ego is wounded if we think we have to bow to anyone and we cannot get it through our egotistical minds that if we are not bowing to God, we are bowing to Satan. God said in Matthew 12:30, "He that is not with me is against me." Now really think about that verse.

There are no in betweens. It's God or Satan. Take your pick. As it is written in Joshua 24:15, "Choose you this day whom ye will serve." And again in Deuteronomy 30:19, "...I have set before you life and death, blessing and cursing: therefore choose life that both thou and thy seed may live."

How do you do that when you don't have faith? "So then faith cometh by hearing, and hearing by the word of God." (Romans 10:17) Hear the Word and take heed to what you hear.

One more thing on which we need to take heed, as regarding what we hear. The Hebrew word 'shema' means 'hear'. In Deuteronomy 6:4 we see this call, "Hear, O Israel: the Lord our God is one Lord." Now that you've heard it, take heed to it. And don't give me that stuff about God is only speaking to Israel or the Jews. If you are a Gentile and are saved, then you are grafted in. (Romans 1:19) And if you are grafted in, then you are spiritual Israel and don't forget, Jesus was a Jew. Not a Baptist, not a Methodist, or anything else, but a Jew. Born and raised a Jew, died a Jew, arose a Jew and will come back as a Jew. Boy! I almost got emotional typing that!

This is an intense beckoning to all the followers of the God of Israel, to hearken to the instructions He has set forth in His Word. It is also a call to the life long obligation to, and blessing of, learning and following God's standards. Take heed with what you are about to hear, even if it is only in the reading of it.

"Hear, O Israel: The Lord our God, is one Lord. And thou shall love the Lord thy God with all thine heart, and with all thy soul, and with all thy might. And these words, which I command thee this day, shall be in thine heart. And thou shalt teach them diligently unto thy children, and shalt talk of them when thou sittest in thine house, and when thou walkest by the way, and when thou liest down, and when thou riseth up. And thou shalt bind them for a sign upon thine hand, and they shall be as frontlets between thine eyes. And thou shalt write them upon the posts of thy house, and on thy gates." (Deut. 6:4-9)

Now, first we are to teach the words to our children, diligently. And just in case you don't have a dictionary, God went on to explain so there would be no misunderstanding. To teach them diligently we must talk of them when we sit in our house. We must talk of them when we walk by the way or when we are moving about. OK. That takes care of two positions. Most people are sitting or walking. So long as we are talking to our children about the marvelous works of God just while sitting or walking, we still have time to run our mouth and have people hearken unto us about getting Mr. Dolittle out of the choir because he wore his tennis shoes to church on Sunday.

Not so, boss. It also says to talk of the works of the Lord when we lie down and when we get up. If you really think about it, that doesn't leave much time to talk about anything else. And guess what? It will be something that we, as the Body, can take heed to. Something we need to hear instead of whether Ms. Do Dad really thinks you bleach your hair and it's not truly blond.

Let's get a life, people. Stop listening to trash and tell the one inserting negative thoughts into your ear to only speak words of the Lord and His grace, or not speak at all. Your ears can get an infection by all the nasty bacteria and it can spread to the whole Body.

Jesus summed it up with, "I have many things to say and to judge of you: but he that sent me is true, and I speak to the world those things which I have *heard* of him." (John 8:26 Italics added) Now how did He hear it? Simple.

He was taught the Torah from day one. "But He was God in the flesh. So He didn't' have to be taught the Word," you say. Oh, yes He did. And the reason I think that is because when He took on a fleshly robe, He literally became a man. Man doesn't know a hill of refried beans (How's that Pastor Hagee, refries?) about the Word when he is born and most of them still don't by the time they die. But you must realize.

Jesus was a Jew. His mother and Joseph were devout Jews and they would have taught Him everything God said to teach our children. They would not have skidded by on that for anything. Therefore, when the Messiah said he would speak to the world those things, which he had heard *of* Him (the Father), I believe He had heard OF the Father from His earthly family. I know two verses down He says He does nothing of Himself, but as His Father hath taught him. How did God choose to teach the Jews?

With the Torah through His Spirit just like we are taught today. And Mary and Joseph would have loved the Torah more than life. Jesus took heed to what He heard. When Jesus was confronted by one of the teachers of the Law, and He was asked which of all the commandments was the most important, He answered, "...The first of all the commandments is, Hear, O Israel: The Lord our God is one Lord: And thou shall love the Lord thy God with all thy heart, and with all thy soul, and with all thy mind, and with all thy strength: this is the first commandment. And the second is like, namely this; Thou shalt love thy neighbor as thyself. There is none other commandment greater than these." (Mark 12:29-31)

This is serious business, folks. I enjoy a good laugh and we try to find humor in most of our bad situations, but sometimes I get scared for people that won't take the Word of God seriously. I look at it this way. We are ambassadors for Christ. That means we are in a foreign country doing a job.

We represent Heaven and we need to be about the Father's business. Why can't we take God at His Word, finish the job and catch the next flight out of here. I'm tired of living out of a suitcase in this sin-infested world. I want to go home. I'm waiting for Him to say, "War's about to break out so it's time to evacuate. Come up hither." Take heed to what you hear so you won't be stuck in the wilderness when He does.

"Hear, O Israel!!!" (Italics added) Take heed to what you hear. Jesus did, that's why He's the Head.

11

My Private Eye Is Watching You

Of the five main senses, sight is the most important. That's spiritually, not physically. The eyes tell you more than taste, touch, hearing and smell and the part of the brain that contains the vision center is bigger than the rest that controls senses.

The eye is a complex structure with three concentric (having a common center) layers of tissue for a covering. The first, which is the tough outermost covering, is called the sclera and it is usually referred to as the 'white of the eye'. The surface is transparent and exposed. This covering is called the conjunctive and it also lines the inside surface of the eyelid. The sclera and conjunctive merge into the cornea. This structure is dome-shaped and is sometimes called the 'window' of the eye.

God chose a really nice location for the vision center of our brain…in the very back. You would think this would make Christians realize that we walk by faith and not by sight. Of course, walking by faith can be sort of scary at times, even when you know God is in control. And I've seen so many Christians that think God will send them out on a limb and then pull out a chain saw.

Sometimes I think God was looking out for our best interest when He put the vision center in the rear. Just think what would happen to you today if we could actually 'see' the things reported seen in the Old Testament. And the only reason we don't is because we have the whole thing backwards. We walk by sight and not by faith.

For instance, let's suppose we were in a country where a major battle was taking place. This hypothetical battle has been raging because the non-believers don't want the believers to have freedom of worship. It's a form of ethnic cleansing thus rendering the country politically correct. Sort of sounds like our country is getting, doesn't it?

Anyway, two believers are trapped in a house and one is not as strong spiritually as the other. They began to pray and the weaker one looks out the window just in time to see the house is totally surrounded. He knows they are going to be killed. Forget that he knelt in supposedly total faith that God would deliver. All he sees is the house surrounded by the enemy.

Falling prostrate on the floor he crawls to his friend and with tears in his eyes he says, "We're surrounded. It doesn't look like God wants us to escape this one."

His friend, who hasn't even broken a sweat over the whole thing replies, "Oh, you're wrong brother, because either we're not looking in the same direction, or you're spiritually blind. Can you not see all the soldiers moving in around our enemy?"

The weaker man takes a second look. Again, he sees only the enemy. The stronger man knows what is wrong, so he looks up toward heaven and makes the request, "Father, open his eyes that he may see what I see."

Immediately, the weaker man's eyes start to see. Soldiers are silently slipping in behind the enemy. They're carrying swords drawn and ready. But instead of attacking, they wait.

The enemy approaches, not even realizing they are being followed with every step. The stronger Christian bows his head and says, "Father, make mine enemies to lay down their weapons and begin to surrender to us and we in turn will begin to bind their hands."

The weak Christian is dumbfounded as he watches each soldier slowly lay down his weapon and they all commence to form a line, each waiting his turn to be bound by the Christians. After the deed is done, the Christians march them into the town where they will be held prisoner. Upon reaching the town and explaining what has taken place, without the aid of Rambo, the prisoners are put behind bars and the Christians are led away...to the funny farm. Why?

They must undergo extensive examinations and psychological evaluations to determine if they are in their right minds. This just doesn't happen in today's world. Diagnosis? *Battle fatigue!* The weaker one was the product of the power of persuasion and the stronger one must have used some kind of gas on the enemy to make them succumb to him and surrender. When questioning the prisoners, they responded they had no choice since they were outnumbered. Mass hysteria, you think?

Go ahead and laugh. You probably thought they would hold their commanding officer spellbound with their story. And if everyone would admit it, as the soldiers began to line up to be bound, you probably thought, "Yeah, right!" But at the same time most of you thinking that way have sat in church and heard a similar story preached from II Kings 6:8-23 and shouted at the faith that was shown.

However, in most of our hearts, we only have faith in what we can see. That is why it is so important to see things as our Head sees them. We must picture in our mind what we are asking the Lord to do. We must see it as though it is already there in the physical realm. It's in the spiritual before it gets to us and we need to visualize it in the physical for it to manifest. It's like this book. I can visualize the cover. I know exactly what I'm praying for. Sometimes I can almost feel the finished product in my hand.

We are not to look at the surroundings and visible obstacles since obstacles are what we see when we take our eyes off the goal, but to the outcome and victory through our Lord. Just think what would have happened to us, the Body, if Jesus had seen us for what we are, instead of what we were to become. Sort of like something my friend, Robert Foster, sent me. (I wonder where he gets all this stuff.)

This is the result of a company profile that could happen if Jesus was trying to start a ministry in today's world and He was trying to do it with His own eyes and what He saw, instead of the way the world thinks it should be. I hope you enjoy this as much as I did.

Subject: Jordan Management Consultants
Company Profile
To: Jesus, Son of Joseph
The Woodcrafter's Carpenter Shop
Nazareth 25922
From: Jordan Management Consultants
Jerusalem 26544

Thank you for submitting the resume of the twelve men you have picked for management positions in your new organization. All of them have now taken our battery of tests, and we have not only run the results through our computers, but also arranged personal interviews for each of them with our psychologist and vocation aptitude consultant.

It is the opinion of the staff that most of your nominees are lacking in background, education and vocational aptitude for the type of enterprise you are undertaking. They do not have the team concept. We would recommend that you search for persons of experience in management ability and proven capacity.

We have summarized the findings of our study below:
Simon Peter is emotional, unstable, and given to fits of temper.
Andrew has absolutely no quality of leadership.

The two brothers, James and John, the sons of Zebedee, place personal interest above the company loyalty.

Thomas demonstrates a questioning attitude that would tend to undermine morale.

We believe it is our duty to tell you that Matthew has been blacklisted by the Greater Jerusalem Better Business Bureau.

James, the son of Alphaeus, and Thaddeus definitely have radical leanings. Additionally, they both registered high scores on the manic depressive scale.

However, one of the candidates shows great potential. He's a man of ability and resourcefulness. He is a great networker, has a keen business mind, and has strong contacts in influential circles.

He's highly motivated, very ambitious and adept with financial matter. We recommend Judas Isacariot as your Controller and Chief Operating Officer. All the other profiles are self-explanatory. We wish you the utmost success in your new venture.

Author Unknown

What if Jesus had chosen the twelve based on the modern method of leadership selection? Most of them would have never had a chance to participate. Jesus chooses people not for who they are, but for what they can become. And that is because He uses His eyesight by faith.

◆   ◆   ◆

In the next few pages we are going to examine the eye and see how it works. There are four groups of disorders for the eyes and after looking at them, we should understand a little more about why God put the vision center in the back of our head and why all the fullness of the God-head was placed in Christ and why He is the Head and we are the Body.

The first disorder is error in refraction. As defined by Webster, refraction is deflection from a straight path undergone by a light ray (Jesus) or energy wave in passing obliquely from one medium (as air, or the Holy Spirit) into another (as glass, or us) in which its velocity is different. Let's do that again.

Refraction: deflection from a straight path undergone by a light ray (Jesus) or energy wave in passing obliquely from one medium (as air, or the Holy Spirit) into another (as glass, or us) in which its velocity is different.

You could think of our whole Body as going through refraction because we're not perfect yet. There are four problems with the eye that are a result of refraction. These problems are nearsightedness, farsightedness, presbyopia, and astigmatism.

Look back at the definition of refraction. Let's put it in real simple form. You've got a light that is passing in a straight line, moved by air. As it hits the eyeball it is deflected or bent, thus entering the eye at a slower speed. This causes problems in focusing on the object.

Genesis 3:1 says, "Now the serpent was more subtle than any beast of the field which the Lord God had made. And he said unto the woman, "Yea, hath God said, Ye shall not eat of every tree of the garden?"

Now look back to Genesis 2:17. In this verse we see that God plainly told Adam not to eat of the tree of the knowledge of good and evil…a direct command. That's about as straight a line of light as you can get. Unmistakable. But notice how farsightedness sets in on Eve in chapter three.

Satan deflected the light by placing doubt in Eve's mind. He asked her, "Yea, *hath* God said" (Italics added) In essence he was saying, "Now, Eve, did God really say that? Just think for a minute. He didn't tell *you* that. He said it to Adam, *if* He said it at all. Maybe Adam retold it wrong?"

So Eve, instead of calling her nearest ophthalmologist or not taking heed to what she was hearing, or better yet, not calling out to God, let the Light be deflected. She even helped it.

She helped it in chapter three verse three, by adding to the Word. "But of the fruit of the tree which is in the midst of the garden, God hath said, Ye shall no eat of it, *neither shall ye touch it,* lest ye die." (Italics added) God never told them to not touch it.

Then to make matters worse, she got someone to sin with her. Verse 6 says, "And when the woman saw that the tree was good for food, and that it was pleasant to the eyes and a tree to be desired to make one wise, she took of the fruit thereof, and did eat, and gave also unto her husband with her, and he did eat." Looks like lust and pride are two good causes of errors in refraction.

The second group of disorders affects the visible eye, which covers one tenth of the surface of the entire eyeball and eyelids, which act as a protective covering. There are several problems that can arise in this group, so I'll only list and describe a few.

Entropion: a condition in which the margin of the eyelid, usually the lower one, turns inward and the lashes rub against the surface of the eyeball. OUCH!!!

Sty: an infected hair follicle.

Conjunctivitis: inflammation of the conjunctive, which is a transparent membrane that lines the eyelids and outer eye to the edge of the cornea.

Iritis: inflammation of the iris or the part of the eye that determines eye color. (I don't think this includes 'pink eye'.)

Cataracts: an opaque or cloudy area that develops on a usually clear lens of the eye. After a period of years, it will block or distort the light entering the eye. Vision is blurry and deterioration is progressive.

There are others but this list can show you the many different ways the visible eye can be affected. However, it seems I hear more about cataracts than any other. As the disorder progresses, it becomes increasingly harder to see because it just keeps getting darker.

Have you ever noticed how many Christians have spiritual cataracts? I love the description given for this disorder: an opaque area that develops over a usually clear lens eventually leading to blockage or distortion of light.

People who suffer from this condition are miserable and if we're not careful, they can be contagious. The light (Jesus) entering the eye is distorted so they have a hard time seeing anything clearly. There is an obstacle in the way, standing between the Light and the point of entry, and obstacles are only things that are seen when you take your eyes off the goal. There are several ways a person can develop spiritual cataracts.

Neglecting to read and study the Word is one. Why is this a prerequisite to spiritual cataracts? Well, to avoid the darkness that sets in. Psalms 119:105 says it this way, "Thy Word is a lamp unto my feet and a light unto my path." Notice anything amazing about that?

Have you ever tried to walk in the woods at night with nothing but a flashlight? If you focus the light on your feet you must consistently look down for the light and you can only see your feet and the immediate area. If you focus the light on the path then you can't see your feet. But the Word shines alllll over the place.

Neglecting to pray is another. How can prayerlessness distort light? Easy. Jesus said in John 8:12 that He was the light of the world and those that follow Him shall not walk in darkness, but shall have the light of life.

Notice the part that says, "...he that followeth me shall not walk in darkness..." To be able to follow someone you must be able to see directly in front of you. There must also be some form of communication. The formula for this communication is as follows:

First, the Father draws us to the Son. John 6:44 says, "No man can come to me, except the Father which hath sent me draw him," and Ephesians 2:8,9 says, "For by grace are ye saved through faith, and that not of yourselves, it is the gift of God: Not of works, lest any man should boast."

Second, the Son bids us follow. Matthew 4:19 reads, "And he saith unto them, Follow me, and I will make you fishers of men. Then in Matthew 8:22, "But Jesus said unto him, Follow me, and let the dead bury the dead.

Third, we make a commitment and confession. "Sirs, what must I do to be saved? And they said, Believe on the Lord Jesus Christ and thou shalt be saved, and thy house." Acts 16:30, 31. Also in Romans 10:9,10 we have, "That if thou shalt confess with thy mouth the Lord Jesus and shalt believe in thine heart that God that raise him from the dead, thou shalt be saved. For with the heart man believeth unto righteousness; and with the mouth confession is made unto salvation."

And fourth, we abide. This involves more than just a confession. A lot of people make a confession without having a possession, and emotion without devotion is just commotion. To drive home this fact we will quote quite a few scriptures.

John 15:1-10: I am the true vine and my Father is the husbandman. Every branch in me that beareth not fruit he taketh a way; and every branch that beareth fruit he purgeth it, that it may bring forth more fruit. Now ye are clean through the word, which I have spoken unto you. *Abide* in me and I in you. As the branch cannot bear fruit of itself, except it abides in the vine, no more can ye, except ye abide in me. I am the vine, ye are the branches: He that abideth in me, and I in him, the same bringeth forth much fruit; for without me ye can do nothing. If a man abides not in me, he is cast forth as a branch, and is withered; and men gather them, and cast them into the fire, and they are burned. If you abide in me, and my words abide in you, ye shall ask what ye will, and it shall be done unto you. Herein is my Father glorified, that ye bear much fruit; so shall ye be my disciples. As the Father hath loved me, so have I loved you. *Continue* ye in my love. *If* ye keep my commandments, ye shall abide in my love; even as I have kept my Father's commandments, and abide in His love. (Italics added)

Having spiritual cataract surgery is necessary to see clearly. This is evident in verse two. The word 'purge' in this verse means to cleanse, and we are made clean by the word. (Verse 3) There are two ways to look at this. One is through salvation.

When someone has physical cataracts the entire lens is usually taken out. Then new lenses are added in the form of eyeglasses, contacts, or a plastic lens placed in the eye at the time of the procedure. II Corinthians 5:17 shows us cataract surgery to produce salvation, sort of like out with the old and in with the new. It says, "Therefore if any man be in Christ he is a new creature, old things are passed away: behold, all things are become new."

The second way to look at this is when a Christian has unconfessed sin in his or her life. In this case, the entire lens does not need to be removed, but only the substance within the lens using a small needle, leaving the transparent capsule of the lens in the eye. Jesus told Peter this during the last supper.

He said in John 13:19, "…He that is washed needeth not save to wash his feet, but is clean every whit; and ye are clean, but not all."

The underlining thought here is picturing a man coming from the public bathhouses and only his feet becoming dirty during the walk. He must then clean his feet. This signifies a daily confessing of our sins so we may abide in the continual fellowship with Christ, thus enabling us to walk in the Light and not in darkness of spiritual cataracts.

Now we come to the third disorder…glaucoma. It is one of the most common severe disorders in the elderly and treatment is vital or it will eventually lead to blindness.

What is it? Well, there is a part of the eyeball called the ciliary body, and it is constantly producing a fluid called aqueous humore. (That's not humor as in funny haha but as in fluid, moisture, and only a doctor would use words like that.)

Anyway, this fluid circulates behind the iris through the pupil and into the compartment between the iris and cornea. If things were normal, it would drain out of the eye through a bunch of tissue between the iris and cornea, which by the way, is intellectually called the drainage angle. From there it goes to a place that leads to a bunch of small veins on the outside of the eye. With glaucoma, it is in this area that we find plumbing problems. The drain doesn't work properly and the fluid flows away more slowly than it is produced or fails to flow away at all. Then we have a build up of pressure. Time to call Mr. Plumber.

Some of the pressure is forced onto a jelly-like fluid that fills the eyeball behind the lens. This pressure on the retina causes the collapse of small blood vessels that feed the cells of the retina and fibers of the optic nerve. Since they no longer have the nourishment needed by the flood supply being shut off, the cells and nerve fibers begin to die. Vision begins to diminish.

Note that. The blood supply is shut off, depriving the retina and fibers of much needed oxygen and nutrients and the nerve fibers begin to die. Remember, the life is in the blood. (Lev. 17:14)

Personally, I think this is the worst disorder of the Body today. Have you ever known people that are so heavenly minded they are no earthly good? These are people that walk around with their hands folded in front of them and every time something goes wrong, they say this is the cross they must bear in life or if someone does something to them, they humbly bow their self-righteous head and in a very soft voice, whisper, "Bless you, my child. All is well." Some people are so humble it makes you sick; especially when they tell you how humble they are.

You see humility is a necessity. But when it doesn't drain right, the pressure builds up. Eventually, you become so pious that you cut off the Blood supply. When you do that, your vision begins to deteriorate and to put it mildly, you die.

I've seen a lot of people commit spiritual suicide by telling others how spiritual they are. They never have a problem that affects their moods. They never take offense when someone speaks falsehoods against them. They always feel the leaders of the church are perfect. They never smile but always seem so solemn. In short, they are boring, and in most cases, to entirely truthful. I've found most men like this are usually short tempered with their wives and most women like this are usually judgmental or perpetual gossips. Most of them are always miserable and they prefer to stay that way.

I picture old movies where the monks are slowly walking around in brown robes and have taken a vow of silence. Do they not realize that is what the devil wants…silence? They act like you're not supposed to tell others of the wonders or saving grace of Christ. Just let them see how humble you are. Laughter is beyond them and they think God never smiles. And do you know why?

They need surgery for glaucoma. The procedure for this is quite simple. It is called an iridectomy and takes about thirty seconds. In this procedure the surgeon makes an incision at the border of the conjunctive and the cornea. A piece of iris is gently pulled through the incision and whacked off. This allows the fluid to drain and relieves the pressure in the eye.

By the way, the iris is a group of radically arranged smooth muscle fibers that make the pupils dilate. Pay attention to your pupils, and you'll notice that if they are of the right size, then the Light is coming in brightly enough. If they are dilated, then you are in lighting that is not so good. Your eyes apparently strain to receive Light. This means you are lacking in sufficient Lighting. Get the picture?

Finally, the fourth group is the back of the eye and eye orbit. The work of the back of the eye is to receive light focused by the front of the eye and change it into nerve impulses. These impulses are then passed along the optic nerve. The optic nerve leads from the back of the retina to the brain. These messages or impulses are passed over this nerve in code and the brain decodes it.

The structure that receives light is the retina, which, according to Webster, is the sensory membrane that lines the eye, receives the image formed by the lens, is the immediate instrument of vision, and is connected with the brain by the optic nerve.

The orbit is the bony socket wherein each eyeball lies. The eye turns in the orbit by muscles attached to the outside of the eyeball and the inside of the socket. Crossed eyes is a disorder cause by an imbalance between these muscles or a defect in the nerves that control them. And this is the disorder we are going to discuss.

Normal eyes will move together. Both will look in the same direction at the same time. This is necessary for clear vision. Without this coordination of both eyes, the eyes are crossed, with one eye looking in one direction and the other looking at something else. In almost all cases (this is adult crossed eyes) there will be double vision. Jesus said in Matthew 6:24, "No man can serve God and mammon." It is dangerous to have your eyes looking at two different objects at the same time. Serious consequences can result. James 1:13-15 explains it best. "Let no man say when he is tempted, I am tempted of God for God cannot be tempted with evil, neither tempteth he any man: But every man is tempted, when he is drawn away by his own lust, and entice. Then when lust hath conceived, it bringeth forth sin; and sin, when it is finished, bringeth forth death."

Think back to a previous chapter where I mentioned one of my neighbors had said the people in church were double minded. This is also double vision or crossed eyes. James 1:8 says, "A double minded man is unstable in all his ways."

The term 'double minded' means two souls and come from the Greek word 'dipsuchos'. This would almost lead one to believe a double minded person has a multiple personality disorder or schizophrenia.

Christ gave us some instructions on how to handle the eye. Matthew 7:5 "...first cast out the beam out of thine own eye; and then shalt thou see clearly to cast out the mote out of thy brother's eye."

However, the eyes also can and will behold great things. Luke 2:30, "...for mine eyes have seen thy salvation."

Luke 10:23, "...blessed are the eyes which see the things that ye see."

Matthew 5:8, "Blessed are the pure in heart: for they shall see God."

I Corinthians 2:9, "but as it is written, Eye hath not seen, nor ear heard, neither have entered into the heart of man, the things which God hath prepared for them that love him."

Then we have the tender loving care God will give to the eyes in the not so distant future. "...and God shall wipe away all tears from their eyes..." Revelation 21:4.

Last of all; let me put one great 'sight' before you. It is the oft-quoted verse of Hebrews 11:1. "Now faith is the substance of things hoped for, the evidence of things not *seen*." (Italics added)

We will constantly have problems if we continue to go by what we see physically. For instance, the following article appeared in our local paper recently and the journalist has graciously consented to let me use it. My hat goes off to Larry B. Littlejohn for his unique sense of humor and the way he sees life.

"Green garden grass snakes can be dangerous. Yes, grass snakes, not rattlesnakes.

A couple in Texas had a lot of potted plants, and during a recent cold spell, the wife was bringing a lot of them indoors to protect them from a possible freeze. It turned out that a little green garden snake was hidden in one of the plants and when it had warmed up, it slithered out and the wife saw it go under the sofa. She let out a very loud scream.

The husband, who was taking a shower, ran out into the living room naked to see what the problem was. She told him there was a snake under the sofa. He got down on the floor on his hands and knees to look for it.

About that time the family dog came and cold-nosed him on the leg. He thought the snake had bitten him and he fainted. His wife thought he had a heart attack, so she called an ambulance. The attendants rushed in and loaded him on the stretcher and started carrying him out.

About that time the snake came out from under the sofa and the Emergency Medical Technician saw it and dropped his end of the stretcher. That's when the man broke his leg and why he was in the hospital. The wife still had the problem of the snake in the house, so she called on a neighbor man. He volunteered to capture the snake. He armed himself with a rolled up newspaper and began poking under the couch. Soon he decided it was gone and told the woman, who sat down on the sofa in relief.

But in relaxing, her hand dangled in between the cushions, where she felt the snake wriggling around. She screamed and fainted, the snake rushed back under the sofa, and the neighbor man, seeing her lying there passed out, tried to use CPR to revive her. The neighbor's wife, who had just returned from shopping at the grocery store, saw her husband's mouth on the woman's mouth and slammed her husband in the back of the head with a bag of canned goods, knocking him out and cutting his scalp to a point where it needed stitches. An ambulance was again called and it was determined that the injury required hospitalization.

The noise woke the woman from her dead faint and she saw her neighbor lying on the floor with his wife bending over him, so she assumed he had been bitten by the snake. She went to the kitchen, brought back a small bottle of whiskey, and began pouring it down the man's throat.

By now the police had arrived. They saw the unconscious man, smelled the whiskey, and assumed that a drunken fight had occurred. They were about to arrest them all when the two women tried to explain how it all happened over a little green snake. They called an ambulance, which took away the neighbor and his sobbing wife.

Just then the little snake crawled out from under the couch. One of the policemen drew his gun and fired at it. He missed the snake and hit the leg of the end table that was on the side of the sofa. The table fell over and the lamp on it shattered and as the bulb broke, it started a fire in the drapes.

The other policeman tried to beat out the flames and fell through the window into the yard on top of the family dog, who startled, jumped up and raced out into the street where an oncoming car swerved to avoid it and smashed into the parked police car and set it on fire. Meanwhile the burning drapes had spread to the walls and the entire house was ablaze.

Neighbors had called the fire department and the arriving fire truck had started raising the ladder, as they were halfway down the street. The rising ladder tore out the overhead wires and put out the electricity and disconnected the telephones in a ten-square city block area.

Time passed. Both men were discharged from the hospital, the house was rebuilt, the police acquired a new car, and all was right with their world.

About a year later they were watching TV and the weatherman announced a cold snap for the night. The husband asked his wife if she thought they should bring in their plants for the night. She shot him.

All because she *saw* a snake.

When it's time to call in the family because the doctors have given up hope, do you *see* the opposite?

When it's time to pay the bills and your checkbook is made of rubber, do you *see* the opposite?

When your children are in total rebellion and the school or court says they're emotionally disturbed and by all rights you should be walking the floor every night…do you *see* the opposite?

If you don't then you are not following II Corinthians 5:7. But Christ does…because He is the Head and He has 20/20 vision.

12

To Think or Not to Think

✦

(That's a Question?)

Have you ever been told you have a one-track mind? I suppose everyone has at some time or another. Webster defines one track as being marked by often narrowly restricted attention to, or absorption in, just one thing.

Do you remember the old movie 'Ozzie and Harriet'? It was about a couple that had two teenage boys named Dave and Ricky. It was one of the programs much like our 'Brady Bunch' of today. You know, the plot always shows the children in some moral dilemma and the parents always have the right answer, the kind of parents that never make a mistake in teaching their children right from wrong and never had to take a class in parenting skills because they never came home from work in a bad mood and always woke up with minty fresh breath?

I was deeply in love with Ozzie and Harriet's son, Ricky Nelson. I just knew that when I grew up fate would bring us together and we would live happily ever after. But alas, he married some chic named Kris. And on national TV, too! The nerve of some people. I'd given him the best years of my life right there in front of the screen and he was cheating on me. Love can quickly turn to hate.

I was devastated!! At the ripe old age of nine I almost lapsed into terminal depression, and when my mother wanted to know what was wrong, she became quite scornful, telling me to stop acting like a child. I was a child! I took a good tongue lashing about fantasies, daydreaming, and the real world. The final blow came when I was accused of having a one-track mind.

I didn't even know what that meant but figured it had to fall right in the same category as my arm obeying her command to pick up my toys. I reasoned this out because her voice had the same overture that signals impatience, followed by disgust then action. With the action something unpleasant always followed.

But to me, it was real. My whole day came to a halt when it was time for Ricky to appear in the living room via television. It was as though regardless of what I was doing at the time, my subconscious took over completely and like a zombie, I mechanically walked to the TV, turned it on and feasted on his face.

There were no visions of us walking down the aisle or selecting a beautiful home and paying cash, or any such nonsense; just blissful ignorance. But through it all, I never had a one-track mind. Actually, nobody has. It is literally, physically impossible, unless you're in a coma and then it's real tricky.

We have three levels of brain activity. The first is the conscious, where you are completely alert and aware of your surroundings and can respond accordingly. The second is our subconscious. This involves things that are existing in the mind but not immediately available to conscious or the mental activities just below the threshold of consciousness.

I like to think this includes major things like singing while you're driving, or minor things like breathing while you're reading. Breathing is a relatively minor thing, don't you think? It's a nasty job, but somehow you have to do it. You see, you're responding without having to think about it.

Can you imagine what John 3:16 would be like if you had to think before you took each breath? Try it. "For God so loved the world (stop, think, breathe deep) that He gave His only begotten Son (stop, think, breathe deep) that whosoever believeth in Him (stop, think, breathe deep) should not perish (stop, think, breathe deep) but have everlasting life." (Stop, think, breathe deep)

Hey! One verse is not so bad but what if you had to do a whole seminar or read a whole book that way? You could faint before you actually remembered to breathe. Worse yet, imagine being in the army in a war under heavy fire and you actually had to think, "Dodge bullet, run, breathe, dodge bullet, run, breathe, dodge bullet." Well, you get the picture.

The third level is unconsciousness. On this level you're unable to perceive or unaware of the happenings around you, thereby rendering you unable to respond to stimuli. This could be any thing from a very deep sleep (such as sleeping through a storm) or being in a coma. Much like what would happen to your husband when you tell him your mother is moving in, thereby rendering him unaware or unable to respond to his surroundings. I enjoyed pulling this trick on my husband from time to time when I needed some time alone. Sent him into withdrawal every time.

Now that you are conscious (no pun intended) of the three levels, let's look at the possibility of having a one-track mind. Again Webster enlightens us, saying the mind is 'the organized conscious and unconscious adaptive mental activity of an organism.' Somewhere, somehow, even though you aren't aware of it, another track is operating, telling you to walk as you cook, continue feeding the baby while on the phone, scratch an itch or turn over while you're asleep. No one can have a one-track mind. In fact, if you did, in all likelihood, you would be dead.

However, let's look at this in a different light. Physically, if this were possible, we know we'd be in a mess. But spiritually, ahhhh, that's a horse of another color. Actually James 1:8 warns us of the need to be just the opposite, saying that 'a double minded man is unstable in all his ways'. Indeed, we are encouraged to strive for a one track mind. Proverbs 3:5 even tells us how to do it. At this point all inquiring minds that want to know will turn to Proverbs and find out how.

You may think it seems like a lot of double talk. First, we are created without a one-track mind, and then God expects us to develop one. Of course! After all, He does claim to choose the foolish things of the world to confound the wise. (I Cor. 1:27) How else can we bring our flesh under subjection? We were created in His image, an identical reflection of Him until sin entered into the world. Now through the blood of Jesus Christ, we can obtain the greatest cloning job every imagined if those of us in the laboratory will only submit to the Great Scientist during the procedure. And remember, we are still examining the reasons why He is the Head and we are the Body.

Every part of the human body is made up of cells. One kind of cell makes blood and another makes bone and another makes skin, etc. Now if every cell wanted to do its own thing, our bodies would be in trouble. Can you imagine the turmoil if our skin cells suddenly decided to do the work of our blood cells?

Of course, this can't happen. However, our cells must be programmed to do particular tasks and since each cell doesn't have a head or brain of its own, the programming must come from somewhere. That's the brain, the one and only built-in computer that no man can duplicate.

No Darwinian imbecile will ever convince me that the big bang started it all. Who put the stuff there for it to ever explode and if we all evolved, when did the evolution stop? If we want children, why go through the pain of childbirth? Just get a monkey, let it keep reproducing several generations and wait for it to evolve into a human. It may take a little longer, but think of the maturity you will have gained and sleep you would not loose while waiting. Of course, during the evolution it might be a little embarrassing to have to explain why your child is the only one with hair all over its body while stepping up to bat and why your child arrived at the ball game swinging from tree to tree instead of in a car like everyone else. Our national laws night consider it a form of child abuse. But you might win in court because it really isn't a child yet; it's just evolving into one.

Why is it when people that believe in reincarnation go to a counselor and get hypnotized and they are taken on a trip of regression to previous lives, NOT ONE has gone back to their original life as a monkey? Are we missing something here or what? Oh, well. It was just a thought.

I might have had some relative swing from a tree by a rope, but I never had one to swing by the tail. Besides, when did that line of thinking stop being a theory and start being a fact? If it's still a theory, then why don't the powers that be let us teach God as a theory? Do they feel threatened? True Christianity promotes love and forgiveness. How can that be a threat? I've wondered off on one of my pet peeves again. No one track mind here.

How does the cells know when to divide and reproduce? How do they know to carry oxygen?

All the duties are carried on without each cell having to take a college course in structural division and distribution. And it comes from the brain. If each cell had its own brain our body parts would soon have to call 911 because of domestic violence. So you can plainly see it is physically impossible for any one to have a one-track mind. Thus it is necessary for the brain to have another part that is responsible for another track.

In an earlier chapter we discussed how the brain is made up of three parts representing the Father, the Son and the Holy Spirit. The second part is called the cerebellum and is responsible for certain subconscious activities, especially coordinating movement, keeping your balance or maintaining your equilibrium.

It would be sort of painful if we tried to walk and could not keep our balance. Same way with serving the Lord. There's no way any Christian can without assistance. You can't do it on your own. You must have something or someone to maintain the balance or you would go off the deep end.

Webster and I are becoming good friends through all this, so once again we'll look to him for definition. The word 'equilibrium' actually comes from two other words. One is 'aequi' meaning weight and the other is 'libra' meaning balance. It is a state of adjustment between opposing or divergent influence or elements, a state of intellectual or emotional balance.

Now I like that! Look at the definition again and let it sink in real slow, kind of saturate your mind. Do the words 'state of adjustment or opposing or divergent influences' sort of leap right out to you? Especially 'opposing influences'? Say the two words slowly, letting them roll off your tongue.

It is my opinion that one reason most people don't live a victorious life in Christ is they don't even realize the depth of the war we are in. This is NOT a street gang scrimmage! This is NOT a police action of the UN. We are in a full-fledged war with the opposing elements or influences. We are in a state of intellectual or emotional unbalance without our cerebellum, which is Christ Jesus. And most people think they are heavily afflicted if they have to work eight hours a day then go home and cook.

If you're having a bad day, why not consider the following:

The average cost of rehabilitating a seal after the Exxon Valdez oil spill in Alaska was $80,000. At a special ceremony, two of the most expensively saved animals were released back into the wild amid cheer and applause from onlookers. A minute later, in full view, they were both eaten by a killer shark.

A psychology student in New York rented out her spare room to a carpenter in order to nag him constantly and study his reactions. After weeks of needling, he snapped and beat her repeatedly with an ax leaving her mentally retarded.

In 1992, Frank Perkins of Los Angeles made an attempt on the world flagpole sitting record. Suffering from the flu he came down eight hours short of the 400-day record. His sponsor had gone bust, his girlfriend had left him and his phone and electricity had been cut off.

A woman came home to find her husband in the kitchen shaking frantically with what looked like a wire running from his waist toward the electric kettle. Intending to jolt him away from the deadly current, she whacked him with a handy plank of wood by the back door, breaking his arm in two places. Until that moment he had been happily listening to his Walkman.

Two animal rights protesters were protesting at the cruelty of sending pigs to a slaughterhouse in Boon. Suddenly the pigs, all two thousand of them, escaped through a broken fence and stampeded, trampling the two hapless protesters to death.

And finally....

Iraqi terrorist, Khay Rahnajet, didn't pay enough postage on a letter bomb. It came back with 'return to sender' stamped on it. Forgetting it was a bomb, he opened it and was blown to bits.

There now!! Your day's not so bad, is it? (Frankly, even with my vivid imagination, I find some of these hard to believe, but they're good for laughs.)

Let's wake up people. This is war and people are dying out there. Don't tell me you are suffering persecution. America hasn't seen persecution yet. We're not even in the firing line yet. We're spoiled rotten and every time God tries to put us in boot camp we want to get a medical discharge and run home to Mama.

It really gets me to hear people talk about how reverent they are but won't sit through the altar call because they are already saved and feel they don't need it. They need it worse because any time a Christian thinks that way, he is headed for a fall, if he even stood up to fall in the first place. The best way to keep your balance is to stay on your knees. The best way to stand up to the devil is to bow down before God.

Most people in our society wouldn't have a clue on how to handle adversity. Once a daughter complained to her father about her life and how things were so hard for her. She did not know how she was going to make it and wanted to give up. She was tired of fighting and struggling. It seemed as one problem was solved a new one arose.

Her father, a chef, took her to the kitchen. He filled three pots with water and placed each on a high fire. Soon the pots came to a boil. In one he placed carrots, in the second he placed eggs, and in the last he place ground coffee beans. He let them sit and boil without saying a word. The daughter sucked her teeth and impatiently waited, wondering what he was doing.

In about twenty minutes he turned off the burners. He fished the carrots out and placed them in a bowl. He pulled the eggs out and placed them in a bowl. Then he ladled the coffee out and placed it in a bowl. Turning to her he asked, "Darling, what do you see?"

"Carrots, eggs, and coffee," she replied.

He brought her closer and asked her to feel the carrots. She did and noted they were soft. He then asked her to take an egg and break it. After pulling off the shell, she observed the hard-boiled egg. Finally, he asked her to sip the coffee. She smiled, as she tasted its rich aroma.

She humbly asked, "What does it mean, Father?"

He explained that each of them had faced the same adversity, boiling water, but each reacted differently. The carrot went in strong, hard and unrelenting. But after being subjected to the boiling water, it softened and became weak.

The egg had been fragile. Its thin outer shell had protected its liquid interior but after sitting through the boiling water, its inside became hardened.

The ground coffee beans were unique however. After they were in the boiling water they had changed the water.

"Which are you?" he asked the daughter. "When adversity knocks on your door, how do you respond? Are you a carrot, an egg, or a coffee bean?"

How about you? Are you the carrot that seems hard, but with pain and adversity do you wilt and become soft and lose your strength? Are you the egg, which starts off with a malleable heart? Were you a fluid spirit, but after a death, a breakup, a divorce, or a layoff, have you become hardened and stiff? Your shell looks the same, but are you bitter and tough with a stiff spirit and heart?

Or are you like the coffee bean? The bean changes the hot water, the thing that is bringing the pain, to its peak flavor as it reaches 212 degrees Fahrenheit. When the water gets the hottest, it just tastes better.

When things are at their worst, we should get better and make things better around us. When people talk about us, does our praises to the Lord increase? When the hour is the darkest and trials are their greatest, does our worship elevate to another level? How do you handle adversity, as a carrot, an egg, or coffee bean?

In trying to adjust or maintain our balance during spiritual warfare it is usually helpful to know our who enemy is. I know a lot of Christians will say that's real easy to figure out. But there are so many that has not let the fact sink in that our enemy is invisible and we need to stop looking at this with the physical eye.

Have you ever wondered about the difference between the kingdom of God and the kingdom of heaven? In Matthew 3:2 John preached, "Repent ye, for the kingdom of heaven is at hand."

The phrase *kingdom of heaven* denotes the Messianic earth rule of Christ, the son of David, and is called the kingdom of heaven, as it is the rule of the heavens over the earth. Daniel 2 explains it as the kingdom which 'the God of heaven' will set up after the destruction by 'stone cut out without hands' of the Gentile world system. The kingdom phases?

First, it is at hand. The phase includes the time element beginning with the ministry of John the Baptist in Matthew 3, to the proclamation of the family or brotherhood in Matthew 12:46-50, to the actual rejection of the King.

The second phase is seven mysteries of the kingdom of heaven that will be fulfilled during this present age as told in Matthew 13. Finally, we have the prophetic phase, or aspect: the kingdom to be set up after the return of Christ as told in Matthew 24.

The kingdom of God is different from the kingdom of Heaven in five ways.

One, it is universal and includes all moral intelligent life that willingly submits to the will of God, while the kingdom of heaven has for its focus the *establishment* of the kingdom of God.

Second, it is entered only by the new birth or being saved and the kingdom of heaven during this time would be the realm of profession as indicated in Matthew 13:1 and Matthew 25:1, 11, and 12.

Third, since the kingdom of heaven is the earthly sphere of the universal kingdom of God, the two have almost all things in common. For this reason many parables and other teachings are spoken of the kingdom of heaven in Matthew, and the kingdom of God in Mark and Luke. It is the omissions, which are significant.

The parables of the wheat and tares and of the net in Matthew 13:24-30, 36-43, and 47-50 are not spoken of the kingdom of God. In that kingdom there are neither tares nor fish. But the parable of the leaven in Matthew 13:33 is spoken of the kingdom of God also, for alas, even the true doctrines of the kingdom are leavened with the errors of which the Pharisees Sadducees, and Herodians were the representatives. The kingdom of God "comes not with outward show" (Luke 17:20) but is chiefly that which is inward and spiritual (Romans 14:17) while the kingdom if heaven is organic, and is to be manifested in glory on the earth. The kingdom of heaven merges into the kingdom of God when Christ, having "put all enemies under His feet, shall have delivered up the kingdom of God, even the Father." (I Corinthians 15:24-28)

In understanding the difference of these two kingdoms, it is also necessary to know *who* the enemy is. Paul said in Ephesians 6:12 that we wrestle against principalities, powers, rulers of the darkness of this world and against spiritual wickedness in high places. It has been my experience that this verse is quoted a lot, but most people haven't taken the time to put it with the phrase 'kingdom of heaven'.

For the next little while, we are going to look at the military kingdom of both Christ and Satan. As it unfolds you will see how, by Christ being the Head, the cerebellum of the brain represents Christ and His help in keeping a balance or equilibrium of the Body. Look at Ephesians 6:12.

"For we wrestle not against flesh and blood but against principalities, against powers, against the rulers of the darkness of this world, against spiritual wickedness in high places." Let me recommend a book for you that will help you get a clear picture of how these evil influences operate in this world. It is 'This Present Darkness' by Frank E. Peretti and published by Crossway Books of Wheaton, Illinois.

I've learned a lot of things in my short (never mind how short) years, like how to cook without the Jolly Green Giant, and how to go snipe hunting (it's a southern joke). I've learned that a catfish is really a dumb creature. Did you know those jokers will eat a nasty little cigarette butt found on the bank quicker that biting the worm? Weird, huh? Okay, back to the point.

By never doing time in the military, I didn't know how the rank ran. For instance, once you got past private, I was lost. You see, in my line of thinking the person that wrote 'Mash 4077' put the wrong rank with certain people. Klinger for example, should have been a major like Frank Burns. Let's face it, would *you* have a surgeon like Frank Burns? Anyway, I had to ask a friend the order of rank.

So looking back at Ephesians we see the order of Satan's army. Remember, he's not the only loony that rebelled. He's the mastermind. Someone had to be in charge of all the arguing between the denominations. So when we read about spiritual warfare we can see that principalities are privates, possibly even corporals and sergeants.

Think about this. I've always been told that Satan cannot be everywhere at once like God. But the first thing people say when something goes wrong is, "The devil is sure riding my back." And this will come from more than one person at a time. How can he do that if he can't be in more than one place at a time?

If Satan is responsible for everything all by him little ole' self then he must be able to move faster than a speeding bullet and leap tall buildings in a single bound. How else could he be the one to throw everyone off balance all at the same time?

Of course, in our present day global society, we are now all suppose to be politically correct. At times I wonder if we still have a military of our own. But in some ways we are still a sovereign country and thank God for a president like President George W. Bush who has the backbone to stand up and say to the UN, "We don't need your permission."

The proper procedure after going through all the channels in our government, would be the President issuing orders to the ones next in line under him. They in turn do the same. This keeps happening until it reaches the sergeant who promptly informs his troops to say good-bye to his family because he is shipping out. We are at war.

During the next while, the lower ranks will be the ones doing the actual fighting, but still the higher ups say *they are* at war. This is true, because someone has to give the orders and make the decisions. The ones that carry out those decisions are the lower ranks or principalities.

Next we have the powers. No private listens to another private. They will, however, listen to the powers that be. Doesn't have to be a BIG power, a sergeant will do. But he's not going to do something that he can order those under him to do. He will also find it disgusting and cowardly to expect those under him to do something that he himself would not do, like fight a war and him go to another country to avoid his duty.

The ones under the sergeant know better than to disobey his orders. So I'd say that gives him a little power. *However…*

He must take orders from someone. He couldn't just issue orders all over the country to every private and corporal to go fight. He has been given orders, too. And he gets those orders from a higher up, or rulers of the darkness of this world.

Now don't get all bent out of shape if you are a higher up. I'm not saying our rulers are of the devil. I'm trying to prove a point here about authority.

Going up the ladder, we see that the higher up one goes, the more authority one has. This is true in the spiritual realms, too. The higher up the imps go, the more authority Satan gives them, until you finally get the king bimbo, the devil himself. That's Satan. Where is his kingdom?

John 12:31 says he is the prince of *this world*. We'll discuss this more in another chapter. But for the moment, if he is the prince of this world, I'd say we are behind enemy lines, wouldn't you? Satan is the prince of this domain and we are being held prisoners. Of course, we will be rescued right before Heaven opens fire on the POW camp.

During a war prisoner are kept in bondage at a prisoner of war camp. They are always looking and waiting for a way out. Usually they call Chuck Norris or Rambo, but this doesn't apply in our situation. It's only when the little imps can't destroy us that Satan himself comes on the scene. As long as we keep our mind and eyes on Christ and listen to the *orders* the Holy Ghost brings back from the Oval Office we are fine.

How do we maintain our balance when we are prisoners of war? How do we keep from giving away vital information when we are tortured? How do we keep our balance mentally, emotionally and spiritually without going over the edge? Just use your HEAD...Jesus!

Let's tackle one balance at a time. (This will help you keep your balance.) Mentally...Romans 12:2 is in the 'survival manual'. It reads, "And be not conformed to this world, but be ye transformed by the *renewing of your mind*. That ye may prove what is that good and acceptable and perfect will of God." (Italics added) How do you transform your mind?

History records certain forms of torture where prisoners are 'brainwashed'. Indeed, I have even met people that say if they listen to certain things long enough, they become brainwashed. Our own son, during his know-it-all teenage years would make intelligent statements like, "Mom, please don't go off on the Bible again. You're brainwashing me."

Frankly, his brain needed washing with all the garbage he was putting in it. He couldn't keep his balance. By putting in the wrong things, like listening to peer pressure and becoming independent, to the point of being independent of God, he couldn't think clearly.

To be accepted he had to dress a certain way, or so he thought. To be accepted, he had to set his own curfew, or so he thought. To be accepted, he should only do his chores if he wanted to and not learn to manage his money, or so he thought. But lo and behold, he soon learned that his *whole* body and not just his left arm, would listen to Mama.

He learned soon enough and never quite forgot that Mama would apply her board of education to his seat of knowledge and his desire to become academically inclined would increase greatly. You must understand that with children, there are three ways for knowledge to enter their brain. One is through the ears, one through the eyes, and the other is through the opposite end of the body. How do we teach our children to maintain balance? With the Word…and a paddle.

And I don't want to hear any of this junk about not spanking a child. It's Bible and I live by it. Yeah, yeah, I know. Everyone loves to quote the verse that says, "Spare the rod, spoil the child." But that's not correct at all. The correct quote is, "He that spareth the rod, *hateth* his son." Did you get that? If you don't spank and correct your children you actually hate them. So don't use the whiny voice with me and say, "Oh, I love my children so much, I hate to see them suffer, especially by my own hand." Fine. But you're living a lie and lying to your children at the same time. According to God's Word, you hate them. Pure and simple.

Freedom of expression is causing kids to go into schools and shoot teachers and other students. Freedom of expression has taught our kids that when they grow up they can sleep around without benefit of marriage and find someone who is compatible. And in seeking our compatibility we now have full blown Aids, and children bearing children only for the grandparents to raise, and slaughter houses for the unborn and a welfare line that is stretching across the globe. By the way, did you know that all the people I know who are for abortion are already born? Don't tell me the powers that be know what's best for our children. They can look at their own statistics and see they FAILED. (Sorry, another pet peeve. I almost lost my balance.)

Emotionally, things rile us. If you deny this, there's something wrong. Everyone at some point or another will get riled to an extent, even my carefully picked heroes. (For those in the dark, that's John Hagee, Creflo Dollar, Frederick Price, Jessie Duplantis, Joyce Meyers and my favorite, my husband.) How do I know this? Well, to me, Gene, my husband is one eighth of an inch from being perfect. He'd almost have to be to put up with me. I know he has faults, somewhere, but he has learned the key to control. And no, the first key is not to get rid of me. He needs me around to prove he has faults.

So let's face it. If *he* has faults it stands to reason my other heroes do, too. Just because they are not as well gifted as I am with faults doesn't mean I should feel superior. Some people were born with a silver spoon in their mouth. I was born with an abundance of faults. But they are still my heroes.

Emotions have more than one kind of eruption. Most people think of rage when we speak of emotions. But there are quite a few. One part of the fruit of the Spirit is temperance. (Gal. 5:22)

Temperance is restraint, moderation in action, thought or feeling. Right above that in verses 19-21 are listed eighteen manifestations of the flesh. If you have ever studied God's numerology, (and we gave a few examples in another chapter) you know that the number eighteen stands for bondage. There's the prisoner of war camp again.

Watch closely. Temperance is one part of the fruit. That means we are to exercise control in everything. However, have you ever tried to maintain control when you've just been delivered of something that has kept you in bondage for years? It's impossible. But God allows us these shows of emotion.

If we kept our balance we wouldn't have to have an eruption of emotions for the flesh. Look at every one of them and see what emotions they produce.

Adultery: produces fear in being caught or fear in losing that which you didn't appreciate to begin with; anger from those you have deceived, guilt, and pain from everyone eventually. This is compounded by the fears of not knowing if your new partner has a sexually transmitted disease.

Fornication: there seems to always be a question as what constitutes adultery and fornication. And the answer would depend on whom you ask. For instance, in our government, (especially during the Clinton administration) at times there seems to be a bit of confusion as to what constitutes sexual relations, so it would only seem natural that they would be confused about the difference between the two actions. So let's go to the final authority on the word fornication and that, my friend, would be the Holy Bible.

Turn to I Corinthians 5. Paul has run into a case of fornication. And fornication can fall into two categories. One is sexual relations between two people that aren't married and the other is incest. In the first verse of chapter five we see our first emotion. Shame!! Shame to the Body for the ones that care about the testimony of the Church. Such shame that it was not even named or mentioned among the Gentiles. That's sick. Keep in mind the Gentiles did not then, nor do they now, have the monopoly on Christianity. Gentiles are proselytes converted into the Messianic Jewish faith where the standards for living a righteous life were first given. And this sin was so bad that even the Gentiles wouldn't mention it and they had no way of knowing how a righteous person was supposed to live until the Jews taught them. Talk about a cell going haywire.

Next verse, next emotion...gloating, strutting their stuff. Can it get any sicker? Could it be these perverts appeared on Jerry Stringer? Instead of the people getting righteous indignation or mourning the backslidden condition of the guilty party, they actually applauded him. I'd say this was malignant cancer, wouldn't you?

"What exactly, was he guilty of," you ask. Incest. The dude went to bed with his stepmother. Did Paul suggest the man and woman have counseling? NO! Did he suggest they have a psychological evaluation to determine why this pervert needed a sexy mother figure or he was deprived of being breast fed at birth? NO! Did he suggest they spend a few days in jail until they paid their debt to society? Come on, people!

It's sin any way you look at it. America is wallowing in it and we don't open our mouths. We're cowards! Sin has been so watered down in our society it doesn't bother us any more. Where are the blushes on the faces of our youth? Gone. Where is the disgust of having more than one sexual partner? It's lost. If God doesn't destroy America, He will owe Sodom and Gomorrah an apology and He doesn't have to ask forgiveness for anything. So watch out. This nation that was founded on the principal of one nation under God now has turned its back on Him and will come to an end.

As a Christian counselor I've had the disgusting opportunity to work with people who were practicing incest. I say disgusting because I haven't met many child molesters or those that practice incest that really want to change. They humbly walk into the office and put on a pitiful face and cry so hard. "I wish I could do better. It's a sickness, you know. Everyone has a weakness. Why doesn't God deliver poor pitiful me from this dreadful illness?"

To which I reply, "It's not an illness, Einstein. It's a sin. You need to repent, submit to God and be led of the Spirit...and by the way, resign your position in the church. I don't want you leading my grandchildren until you've been totally delivered of this."

The Body has allowed sin to come in so much that we have developed a tolerance and become immune. We no longer want to say anything because, "Well, Sister, we must remain humble and above all, we shouldn't judge." To which I say, "Excuse me. But we need to look at the Word a little deeper. Did you know the longer we allow the mess to go on in the Body the more we become addicted?

It's just like drugs. The more we see and allow, the more we want, and the higher our tolerance rate and the less it bothers us.

I Peter 4:17 says, "For the time is come that judgment must begin at the house of God and if it first begin at us, what shall the end be of them that obey not the gospel of God?" But let's not leave the next verse out because it is definitely food for thought. Verse 10 says, "And if the righteous scarcely be saved, where shall the ungodly and the sinner appear?" *If the righteous scarcely be saved.* Let's repeat that and let it sink in real deep. If the RIGHTEOUS SCARCELY be saved. And we strut around thinking we are so godly. Look at it!! WE are the RIGHTEOUS and WE are SCARCELY saved.

That scares me. Where is America's fear of God? We've taught so long on the love that we have neglected to remind the people He is also just and He said to be a peculiar people, to abstain from the very appearance of evil, to come out from among them. In other words, we don't mind getting our righteous robes dingy. We don't want any spots or blemishes, but we tolerate the dinginess. A spot or blemish sticks out and is very noticeable but dinginess kinda blends in and has an overall appearance so that it is really not that noticeable.

Jesus is going to return someday and personally, I think it is so close, if we listen good, we can almost hear the silverware rattling on the table for the marriage feast of the Lamb. He will return and judge the whole earth and set up His kingdom, ruling and reigning from Jerusalem. What kind of order will He have? A new order? No. If God is the same yesterday, today and forever, then the order God has always had, will be re-established.

People tell me you can't mix politics and religion. I've even had some of the Body toss smart-alec remarks about it with their ever so humble attitude of, "Well Sister, I don't believe in mixing the two. I just believe in serving the Lord."

Excuse me, Florence Nightingale. But when Christ returns He will be crowned the King of Kings and what does a King do? He rules. Politically. You don't rule by building one's self esteem. You rule by authority and authority means commands. And commands means ruling. King means in charge. You're the Boss. It's not like our country where we have a democracy and something is determined by vote...well, sometimes it is. A king makes the decisions and the decisions are carried out, regardless. Even Jesus taught to purge the evil from among us. Matthew 18 is an excellent place to learn of how to take care of problems and differences in the congregation.

So why do we do it? Why do we continue to let problems fester and grow until we have a full-fledged infection on our hands? It's because we have become immune to sin.

The Body is very sick. You could almost say we are bordering on the verge of Aids. This disease does not kill a person. It attacks their immune system and leaves them open to all the other life threatening diseases. They cannot fight them off.

There is an herb called Echinacea. This is a very powerful herb and is used to boost the immune system. The Body of Christ needs a boost. Our system is so worn down by sin; we have heaped upon ourselves teachers with itchy ears saying only what we want to hear and living our lives as though we have no problems, as though there is no absolute right or wrong. We need a triple dose of Echinacea in the form of convictions and repentance and Godly backbone.

Can you guess how many friends I have? Moving on….

Uncleanness: Debauchery, extreme indulgence in sensuality, orgies. The emotions produced…fear. Fear of pregnancy, fear of being caught, fear of disease, tension from not being accepted, insecurity, or else you would be satisfied with one partner.

Lasciviousness: licentiousness, lacking legal or moral restraints; disregarding sexual restraints. Emotions produced are the same as uncleanness.

Notice all of the first four manifestations are against the human body. One interesting note is in I Cor. 6:18 where Paul says that every sin a man doeth is without the body; But he that committeth fornication sinneth against his own body.

Idolatry: I Samuel 15:23 tells us that stubbornness and idolatry go hand in hand. Same thing. In Leviticus 18:21, 20:2-5, Deut. 12:31, 18:10, II Kings 3:26-27 and Psalms 106:37 to name just a few. We read of the practice of human sacrifice in idolatry. Now use your imagination. If you were practicing idolatry with the ritual of offering human sacrifice, which emotions do you think it would arouse?

I guess it would depend a lot on whether you were the sacrificer or the sacrificee. Either way would call for a highly eruptive emotion. But we have other forms of idolatry if we would only admit it. Look at how we practice idolatry. Without naming any names, let me share this with you.

A few years ago a man was tried and convicted of misappropriation and fraudulent gain of funds within a ministry. This man was given a sentence of twenty-five years. While in the same state, a man got angry with his child and drowned it and he was only given two years. Now somebody sit there and tell me that is justice. Somebody tell me our country is not practicing idolatry with money. When the taking of a life, especially that of a defenseless child, carries less punishment than the taking of one's money, something is wrong and we are practicing idolatry. And it is our fault because we do not stand up and demand justice.

Witchcraft: Again we go to I Samuel 15:23. Witchcraft is listed as being the same thing as rebellion. Emotions evoked are fear, anger, pride, confusion, resentment, and short-term false state of peace.

An interesting note. Remember we saw the first four manifestations of the flesh were sins against the body? These sins involve a physical decision followed by action. The last two discussed, idolatry and witchcraft involve a spiritual decision and action against the Most High God. The next eight are emotions within themselves not requiring an actual physical or mental movement, but simply emotions against our own mind.

Hatred: As I said these are emotions within themselves. But if you are harboring this manifestation of the flesh, it will keep you out of fellowship with God, big time. It brings on actions that should be left undone in little ways we refuse to see. And there is a very thin line between love and hate.

Variance: means contention, strife, quarreling. Let's see. Results are anger hate, fear, pride, emotional pain, confusion, doubt. Need any more?

Emulations: to make one jealous. Now there's an emotion to describe the meaning of the word. And of course jealousy brings confusion, doubt, anger, hate.

Wrath: to get revenge. This emotion brings on an emotion called satisfaction. Satisfaction is not always healthy and when obtained in this manner can leave a lot of loose ends.

Strife: This pretty much speaks for itself. However, let me insert one thing. If you are at strife it means you are struggling, not necessarily fighting physically. You can struggle with emotions, bills, sickness, etc. Where is the peace when these things beset us?

Seditions: to separate or incite a riot. To separate could fall under the category of gossiping. This evokes anger, hate, and confusion. Do you get the impression all the actions go together and may be hazardous to your health?

Heresies: Webster says it's an opinion or practice contrary to church dogma, and opinion contrary to the TRUTH. A lot of people get bent out of shape when you tell them the truth. Like when you tell a homosexual God did not make them that way. Anger, he needs someone to blame it on. And when you tell the sexually active they need to be married first. Anger. And when you tell the church members they are supposed to tithe and it wouldn't hurt to give a little extra as an offering, because God said we have robbed Him in both ways. (Mal. 3:8) Anger. The truth hurts, but the truth will make you free. (John 8:32)

Envyings: Jealousy. Manifest anger, emotional hurt, hate, coveting.

The last ones go back to the physical again requiring decisions and physiccal action against mankind.

Murders: Whoa!! This can evoke a lot of emotions and I think the worse murder is the one using the tongue as the weapon. This is a murder that last a lifetime. The victim is constantly dying but never dead. Can't breathe, can't die. And the perpetrator usually gets off scott free with our law. But there's a better judgment day coming, and a just judge will sit on the bench.

Drunkenness: Confusion, anger, hate, jealousy, stupidity, (whoops! That's a characteristic and action, not an emotion.) Short term false joy, and to the one at home suffering, it brings about a lot more. To the ones laid to rest in the cemetery I hope they found Christ and felt forgiveness and humility.

Revellings: Noisy party and merry making according to Webster. According to Young's Concordance it is wantonness or unruly, hard to control. In other words a Saturday night brawl. I would say this calls for strong emotions.

And such like: Boy! God sure covers all the bases doesn't He? This can encompass a wide variety of things…and emotions.

Considering how all these extracurricular activities will keep your stomach in a knot, why do people insist on doing them? They've lost their balance. Go back once more and read Galatians 5.

Notice something interesting? There are eighteen manifestations of the flesh. There are nine parts to the fruit of the Spirit. That means the scale is tipped in the wrong direction if you consider the weight since there are twice as many of the flesh than the Spirit. This tells me the devil is not as self-confident as he wants you to think because he has to have twice the reinforcements. It also tells me that little is much when God is in it.

How do we maintain our balance? Ephesians 5:18 says, "…be filled with the Spirit." That's one way. But I also like Psalms 119:105. "Thy Word is a lamp unto my feet and a light unto my path.' Common sense tells you that if you walk in the dark you might stumble. That's why we have street lamps. But you can walk anywhere, any time you want with the Word and you will always have a light. How do we maintain emotional balance? With the Word.

Last, but not least…spiritual balance. Hard. You betch ya. Tiring? Indeed it is. Frustrating? Uh-huh. Does victory ever come? OH YEAH. But James 4:7 gives us the two techniques used for victory and in the precise order they are to be used. "Submit yourselves therefore to God. Resist the devil and he will flee from you." Submit in one direction, resist in the other. The techniques sound so simple; putting them into practice takes a little effort and a lot of prayer. Prayer needs faith and faith cometh by hearing and hearing by the Word. (Romans 10:18) So how do we maintain spiritual balance? With the Word.

Now you may feel as though I'm telling you to read and study all the time. Not necessarily, because we are also told to be doers of the Word and not hearers only. Then how do we always maintain with the Word? Simple.

St. John 1:1 tells us, "In the beginning was the Word, and the Word was with God, and the Word was God. The same was in the beginning with God." This is talking about a literal person and it is also talking about the spoken Word. In order for us to maintain balance we must abide in the Word. John 15:3-4 explains it beautifully. "Now ye are clean through the Word which I have spoken unto you. Abide in me, and I in you. As the branches cannot bear fruit of itself, except it abide in the vine; no more can ye, except ye abide in me."

How clear, how simple, how relaxing and peaceful to know that all my problems are taken care of if I just abide. When Satan tells me I'm a failure, I abide. When the bills are due, I abide. When I feel as though no one cares, I abide. When I'm on an emotional roller coaster, I abide.

My Cerebellum never suffers from a messed up equilibrium. He never suffers from fluid in the inner ear because He only hears what the Father tells Him. As long as I trust in the Lord with all my heart and lean not unto my own understanding and acknowledge Him in all my ways, He will direct my paths. He will coordinate my every move and I'll not get in my own way if I let Him do His job. It's when I try to do it for Him that I lose my balance.

13

We're So Modern And
He's So....

Primitive:

That's the word used to describe the brain stem. So if I'm talking about a thing such as the brain stem, why does the title of this chapter say, "He?"

Simple. We're still comparing the Head and the Body. Remember at the beginning we discussed how the brain is divided into three major parts? We've already shown how the first part represents the Father because it is in two parts and Jesus said, "I and my Father are one." (John 10:30)

The second part of the brain, the cerebellum, represents Christ. The third part, the brain stem, represents the Holy Ghost and the Lexicon Universal Encyclopedia says the brain stem is the most primitive structure of the brain. That thrilled me. And do you know why? Because it just proves all the more that the Bible is the Word of God. How?

The Bible says God is a Spirit. (John 4:24) It also says in Genesis 1:2 that the Spirit of God moved upon the face of the earth. Then in Genesis 1:26 it tells us that God said, "Let us make man in our image."

Notice the plural forms of the pronouns. It's us, not me. It's our, not my. Now is it me or does it appear there was more than one Person there for the first Earth Summit on cloning?

But the really fascinating part of it all is that my good ole' buddy Webster recognizes this concept, too. He says in his much published book, the dictionary, the word 'primitive' means not derived, original primary, assumed as a basis. By the dictionary's own words we see the Spirit of God was always there. Original primary, not derived. Man, I like that!

The brain stem has as its major function, control of our breathing and circulation. In Genesis 2:7 we see the first CPR. I can't help but contemplate on the Tower of Babel at this point.

Look at Genesis 11. Verse 1 says, "And the whole earth was of one language, and of one speech." Sort of like our computers of today that translates the language. Verse 2: "And it came to pass as they journeyed from the east that they found a plain in the land of Shinar, and they dwell there." Now it starts to pick up and gives a perfect picture of perpetual backsliding. They started journeying *from* the east.

The reason I see it as perpetual backsliding is because the East holds great significance concerning our Head. When they started moving away from the east they began to loose direction. It was standard practice to face the rising sun when determining direction and the sun rises in the east. Likewise, when we face the risen Son we can determine the right direction. These nuts walked *away* from the Son. Even the tabernacle in the wilderness faced the east.

We also know that Jesus is going to split the eastern sky when He returns. (Matthew 24:27) There is even a song that says, "Keep your eyes upon the eastern sky, lift up your heads, redemption draweth nigh."

Did you know that the Lord returning has such great significance that in one particular county in North Carolina, when you bury someone in a private church cemetery, the coffin is placed facing the east? I guess they figure if the person were saved, they would have an easier time seeing Jesus during the resurrection. Personally, I feel it doesn't make any difference what direction the old body is buried because it will come up regardless and the Bible says every eye shall see Him. (Rev. 1:7)

So we see as soon as we start to journey away from the Son we take our first step toward backsliding. But that's not the worst part. Look at the rest of verse 2. Not only did they walk away from the east, they found a place they liked and decided to stay. Oh, how beautiful sin will look when we can't see the Son.

Verse 3. "And they said one to another, Go to, let us make brick, and burn them thoroughly. And they had brick for stone, and slime had they for mortar." Soon they began to do what all-good church members do. They decided they could do it alone. Can't you just hear them talking quietly among themselves?

"Look what we've done. We've come this far all by ourselves. No help from anyone. Ain't we someum?"

Verse 4: "And they said, Go to, let us build us a city and a tower, whose top may reach unto heaven; and let us make us a name, lest we be scattered abroad upon the face of the whole earth." In today's church language it would read something like this:

"And since we been here so long and we've done just fine without any help, and we don't need anyone coming in telling us we need to learn to give God the glory, we just gonna build another church and show 'em we can do it. And when we make a name for ourselves, thata show 'em."

Verses 5-8: "And the Lord came down to see the city and the tower, which the children of men builded. And the Lord said, Behold, the people is one, and they have all one language; this they begin to do; and now nothing will be restrained from them, which they have imagined to do. Go to, let us go down, and there confound their language, that they may not understand one another's speech. So the Lord scattered them abroad from thence upon the face of all the earth; and they left off to build the city."

In today's church language it would read something like this: And the Lord came down and said, "Oh, no, you don't."

Let's face it. They blew it at the Tower of Babel and they're gonna blow it again. Have you ever wondered, if *our* brain is all we need, and there is no God, and our essence is within ourselves, and because we are *soooo* smart we do not need a God, why do we activate the lungs and heart first at birth? It's because our brain couldn't even function until we get the lungs in third gear. Why don't we say, "Baby, breathe". Of course, the human race would have been mere zombies if we did; walking dead men, like most of the people today. But if we are so smart we don't need the presence of a God, why do we insist on using our lungs and heart first? Why not the brain?

Even the atheists have to admit that the brain cannot function without air, therefore the lungs had to get their engines started first. Stop the flow of blood and air and see how quick the brain goes ballistic. So why?

It's because of the Holy Ghost. Even Jesus couldn't live without Him. We have an account of this in Matthew 27:50 and I would think that when He yielded up the Ghost, He ceased to exist in this body as we know it. I like to think that on the day of His resurrection He ecstatically welcomed His Spirit back into His body. What's the Holy Ghost got to do with us breathing, or our heart and circulation?

In a previous chapter we discussed the life being in the blood and Jesus breathing on the disciples and telling them to receive the Holy Ghost. Now we may ask why He had to breathe on them *again* so long after God breathed the breath of life into Adam in the Garden.

Picture it this way. Adam was created. God gave him breath and life. Adam breathed long enough to sin and when he did, he had an allergic reaction to the fruit and went into respiratory arrest. Instantly his brain was deprived of air and he died. Spiritually.

In order for man to come back to life, he had to be given the Breath of Life. Jesus performed CPR again and the Body has been breathing fine ever since. Please review that chapter to refresh your memory and tie in what you've read with this. It makes this all the more beautiful.

Since the brain stem controls the function of the lungs and heart, and represents the Holy Ghost, I'd like to start with the lungs first. The reason for this is that if all God had to do was breathe and man became a living soul, that meant man's blood was already there. God created it and installed it but it was just kinda laying there, lifeless. It took the breath to get it circulating and we've already seen that the breath is the Holy Ghost. Sort of like the energy from a battery when we jump-start a car. So it would appear that the heart and blood is nothing without air. Actually, it's obvious because God said the life is *in* the blood and it's the Holy Ghost that preserves us. Due to this statement made by God, it would be impossible for a person to *bleed to death*. It's not the blood in our bodies that keep us alive, but the life that's *in* the blood. The blood is only a vehicle to transport life. Moving on…

The Respiratory System: It is comprised of the nose, throat and trachea, or windpipe. Inside the chest the windpipe separates into two main tubes. Each one goes into one lung each and divides again. This time it divides into smaller air passages and at the tip of these smaller passages is a cavity much like a balloon.

This cavity is called the alveolus, and each lung contains approximately 300 million of these cavities. It is there, in the hidden confines of the lungs that the vital exchange of oxygen and carbon dioxide takes place through the tiny blood vessels in the thin walls of the alveoli.

A person's heart is the center of the circulatory system and it pumps approximately five quarts of blood (five is God's number for grace) in a complete circuit through the body every minute. It has two pumps located side by side. The one on the right side pumps blood to the lungs where waste gases like carbon dioxide are removed and oxygen returns to the pump on the left side where it is moved out into the rest of the body.

Blood will flow away from the heart, either to the lungs or the rest of the body, through the first set of vessels called arteries and these vessels keeps branching off into smaller vessels repeatedly until they become very tiny and are called capillaries. Throughout this whole system, your blood delivers oxygen and nutrients to your tissues and picks up waste.

This process is finished in the capillaries and as the blood moves through on its way back to the heart, the vessels gradually get bigger until they become veins. From there the blood is carried through the organs and collects the waste and heads back to the heart. Then the process starts again. Can't you just hear the blood cells moaning as they return to the starting point while carrying all that waste? "Yuck, what a mess. I need a bath. This stuff is nasty." Then when it's finished the process and starts all over you can hear the sigh of relief with the very first pump, "Wheeeeee."

Since death was passed on to all men for that all have sinned (Romans 5:12), we need to examine the heart very closely. The word 'heart' is used in the scriptures a total of 918 times. Woven into all this are comprehensive descriptions and functions of the heart. The following list will show you all the descriptions of the Christian heart if the Spirit leads them:

Broken—Psalms 34:18	Pure—Proverbs 22:11; 6:1
Clean—Psalms 73:1	Regenerated—John 3:3
Compassionate—Lam. 3:51	Sincere—Eph. 6:5
Contrite—Psalms 57:17	Sorrowful—Proverbs 15:13
Enlightened—II Corinthians 4:6	Sound—Proverbs 14:30
Fixed—Psalms 57:7	Strengthened—I Thess. 3:13
Holy—I Peter 3:15	Tender—Psalms 22:14
Joyful—Psalms 97:11	Understanding—Proverbs 15:14
Merry—Proverbs 15:13	Upright—Psalms 125:4
Perfect—Psalms 101:2	Wise—I Kings 4:29
Prepared—Proverbs 16:1	Zealous—Jeremiah 20:9

Notice there are 22 descriptions of the Christian heart. Let's take another look at God's numerology. Twenty-two stands for "Light Making Manifest'. By the way, let me recommend a book that will enlighten you on the subject. It is 'The Arithmetic of God' and Don Kistler, whom has now gone on and is probably kicking up gold dust on the streets of Glory right now, penned it.

♦   ♦   ♦

Now for the un-regenerated heart. It is:

A fountain of evil—Mark 7:21	Lustful—Ezekiel 11:21
Blind—Ephesians 4:18	Malicious—Proverbs 24:2
Contains evil thoughts—Matt 15:19	Proud—Psalms 101:5
Covetous—II Peter 2:14	Sensual—Hosea 13:6
Deceitful—Jeremiah 17:9	Stony—Ezekiel 11:9
Diabolical—Acts 5:3	Subtle—Proverbs 7:10
Foolish—Proverbs 22:15	Wayward—Psalms 101:4
Hard—Psalms 76:5	Wicked—Jeremiah 17:9
Impenitent—Romans 2:5	Worldly—Acts 8:21, 22
Loves Evil—Psalms 95:10	

There are 21 descriptions listed above for the un-regenerated heart. The number 21 stands for "Exceeding Sinfulness of Sin."

♦   ♦   ♦

The functions, or duties of the heart, are listed below:

It is foremost the center or seat of affections. Deuteronomy 30:6
It should be devoted. (To the Right Person) Psalms 4:4
It should exhibit faith. (In the Right Person) Psalms 112:7
It should exhibit fear of God since according to Proverbs 1:7, fear is the beginning of knowledge.
It should be graciously affected by God. I Samuel 10:26
It should render unto God due fidelity. Nehemiah 9:8
It should render unto God obedience. I Kings 2:4
It should be repentant. Psalms 51:17
It should seek God. Psalms 10:17
It should exhibit trust in God. Proverbs 3:5

There are ten functions of the heart. The number ten stands for the Law.

◆   ◆   ◆

The heart is also capable of several other things.

The heart can speak. Matthew 12:34 and Psalms 14:1
The heart can think and has intentions. Hebrews 4:12
The heart is secretive. Psalms 44:21
The heart is used as a tablet for writing. Romans 2:15
The heart is exposed. I Samuel 16:7
The heart will lie. Proverbs 21:2
The heart is vulnerable. Proverbs 4:23

Notice the heart has seven other capabilities. The number seven stands for completeness. Now you may ask how the stem with its control of the heart and lungs represent the Holy Ghost. Look at it this way. The life is in the blood and if we try to circulate our own blood, we die. John 3:5 explains, "Jesus answered, Verily, verily I say unto you. Except a man be born of water and of the Spirit, he cannot enter into the kingdom of God."

And in Romans 7:14-25 we read how Paul tells of the struggle he has with sin and trying to keep clean spiritually. He says he wants to do good but no good thing dwells within him and if he does that which he does not want to do, it is not him but the sin that dwells within him that does it. He explains there is a law in his members warring against the laws of the mind and bringing him into captivity to the law. He sums it up by saying that with his mind he serves the law of God and with the flesh the law of sin. What we must always struggle to do is overcome the flesh.

When Jesus told the disciples He would go away and then He would send a Comforter, He gave specific duties the Holy Spirit would be responsible for. His responsibilities are:

He will dwell with, and be in, Christians. John 14:17
He will teach Christians all things. John 14:26
He will remind us, or bring all things to our remembrance. John 14:26
He will testify of the Christ. John 15:26
He will reprove the world of sin, righteousness and judgment. John 16:8-11.
He will guide us into all truth. John 16:13
He will not speak of Himself, but only what He shall hear. John16:13

He will show us things to come. Boy!! Let somebody in most of our churches of today say anything about being shown things in future events and the church is ready to excommunicate them or burn them at the stake. But nowhere in this chapter does Jesus say it would only last through the first twelve disciples. John 16:13

He will glorify Jesus. John 16:14

Isn't that amazing? Jesus listed nine specific instructions for the Holy Spirit and that just happens to be the same number of fruit.

We said earlier that the human heart is the center of the circulatory system. One side pumps blood into the lungs where an exchange of gases (replacing carbon dioxide with oxygen) takes place. Paul said in Romans 12:2, "And be not conformed to this world: but be ye transformed by the *renewing* of your mind." (Italics added)

Your brain is not your mind. It is a muscle just like the others. Your mind is your heart, your seat of emotions, and your will. The only way you can renew your mind is to let the Holy Spirit control the heart and lungs. Through His control your heart will pump the Life into the same lungs Jesus breathed life into when you accepted Him as your Savior.

The lungs will turn away the old air or old sinful nature and take in the *'life giving air'*. The sacred blood will be carried through your body. Jesus said in John 6:63 that it is the Spirit that quickens and the flesh profits nothing. He also said the words He speaks to us are spirit and life.

Picture your mind like a computer. The computer will only put out what has been programmed in. People must write programs and put them into the computer before it will tell us anything. Your mind, before rebirth, was full of garbage. You must take it out (the lungs exhaling) and put in the good (the lungs inhaling)

Jesus said, "Now ye are clean through the word which I have spoken unto you." (John 15:3) Take in God's Word and your blood and lungs will be filtered like you've never seen before. It's a great way to detox.

14

The Nerve of Some People

I'm sorry it's taken so long to write this segment of the book. Hope I didn't keep you waiting too long but there were things going on at church and I just had to help the kids in the selection of their new home. (They still value Mom's opinion…ain't that great?) Then I had to get back into the line of thinking in order to write and that takes a while. Kinda like a movie I watched the other night about an author and as he sat down to write, he just stared at the page. My husband laughed and said, "Look familiar?"

I have to admit this part was catchy. When I started this particular area, I just knew the answer was obvious. But alas, I learned that God is very complex and at the same time, so simple. There were moments during the research that I actually pictured Him sitting up there chuckling to Himself about my confusion. By the way, I do believe God has a sense of humor. After all, He created me.

We've already learned that the brain is divided into three parts. But to think, feel or act without a body is as reasonable as trying to eat without a mouth or sneeze without a nose. When our children were small we developed our own family traditions for holidays. For instance, Thanksgiving was not always celebrated with a turkey for dinner…(actually the turkey usually had other plans and would not accept our invitation). Nor did we feel as though this was the only day of the year to be thankful. If you can't be thankful every day, why be hypocritical on the fourth Thursday of November?

I used to love our family reunions because at least one day out of the year I could still play my mind games with people. You've probably figured out that I have somewhat of an attitude with certain situations. So each year when everyone would squeal and run to hug my neck saying how they had missed me *soooo* much, I would squeal right back and say, "I *knooooow*…that's why you never bothered to answer my letters or get in touch with me." Needless to say, I haven't been notified of one in quite a while.

Our family would find something to celebrate and be thankful for all the time. Good report cards or improvement in grades, little league baseball games, finishing the track race after the doctor said the asthma was too bad, etc. We even celebrated Father's Day one week late this year because we wanted all the fathers present, which included my husband, our sons, and their families, plus our sons' fathers-in-law. After all, these gentlemen gave us two of the best daughters-in-law anyone could imagine so it's only natural we ask them to help celebrate.

Anyway, Christmas was always a wonderful time because the boys never knew how we would celebrate. Sometimes, it would be laughter after they open all their gag gifts. Sometimes it would be a solemn occasion as we presented the glorious birth of our Lord and explained that this Christmas, even though they knew all presents were a gift from God, this time He wanted us to give them the best gift of all…the knowledge of Jesus and His plan for salvation.

One hilarious Christmas we had gotten our youngest his heart's desire which was a go-cart. When he came down the hall, he saw it immediately where my husband had slipped it in through the night and put it under the tree. Our eldest, however, wanted a white guitar, so instead of putting it under the tree, Gene hid it right in front of the refrigerator, which, incidentally, was also white. We knew Tony was a sleepy head and took a while to get going in the mornings.

As they came in Joe's eyes lit up with joy and yelling, "All right!" he ran to the go-cart. Tony looked around for his gift but being the easygoing guy he was, did not say a word when he didn't see it. We waited, and although we could tell he was disappointed, he never said a word. Finally Gene said, "Son, you need some juice to wake up. Go into the kitchen and get a glass to get you started before breakfast."

Tony obediently got up, went into the kitchen, moved his guitar out of the way and got a glass of juice. It was only after he had returned and taken a few sips that it registered. Honestly, I didn't know the boy could move that fast that early in the day, and although we listened to wrong chords for several months, we can now say we feel he's among the best. Way to go, Tony!

Another example was the year our eldest was to turn sixteen. My husband purchased a used truck and for six months our son was told to fix it up any way he thought his dad would like it. He was allowed to spend a certain amount of money for this project, which included a paint job, new wheels, a sound system…all the works.

Of course, being the observant parents we are, we knew he would buy things *he* liked and later try to convince his dad that it was all for him. Imagine his surprise when, on his birthday, we handed him the key to the truck with a full tank of gas. Imagine our surprise when he came home that night with his first ticket. Imagine the magistrate's surprise when he smugly paid the whole thing with 3200 unwrapped pennies. Ain't life grand?

That's pretty much the way it's been during my search. Don't get me wrong. I learned a lot, met some of the most interesting people and had a thoroughly great time. I knew sooner or later God would show me what I needed to know and in the meantime, He and I enjoyed one long Christmas.

In an earlier chapter we discussed how the nervous system is divided into two parts: the central nervous system, being a part of the Head and the peripheral nervous system being a part of the Body. This knowledge gave the incentive to study a bit further once I saw how fascinating the comparisons were to the parts of the brain, *our* head and *His* head.

That's when it sunk in that we have twelve cranial nerves, and they arise from the lower surface of the brain and pass through openings in the skull to the periphery of the body. Now since there are twelve of these babies, I automatically thought they represented the twelve disciples. And then something else happened that confirmed it as far as I was concerned.

I met a doctor during one of my mother's numerous visits that told me she thought an embryo had a nerve connected with the eye that would eventually dissolve during gestation. So it seemed this would make thirteen nerves instead of 12, which account for Judas Iscariot committing suicide and the addition of Matthias after the ascension of Christ. Unfortunately I could not find any material to verify it and for some reason, these doctors around here don't want to give out any information unless you're pre-approved by your HMO.

Then I thought they might represent the twelve tribes of Israel. So I went through the process of evaluating each name of every son of Jacob, its meaning and their personality traits, then comparing it to the name of each nerve and its function. Nothing matched. And to make matters worse, during all this reading, I discovered the twelve nerves are actually twenty-four because these little dillies come in pairs. By this time, it's like, "Come on, Lord. Give me a little help here. There has to be a connection somewhere." And help me He did.

Let me give you some background information here. We've discussed at great length all the parts of the brain and their functions. But in order for a brain to have any effect on the body it must send messages and the messages must correctly reach the targeted area for the body to respond. How does the brain get the messages to the designated area? Through the nerves.

I never could understand why a person with *bad nerves* would always go to a psychologist instead of a neurologist. Seems to me the *nerves* aren't bad but something is blocking the message coming from the frontal lobe that governs the personality and the fruit of the Spirit is not showing forth. Remember, one of the parts of the fruit is faith. I realize the phrase *bad nerves* is just our terminology, but to me it's a wrong one.

The way I see it, we have a very mixed language. Some of our words are used in wrong places and our words are so important. I feel we should say what we mean and mean what we say. Recently, in a small hamburger joint, I overheard a customer say to the waitress, "I'd like to get a fast hot dog, please." The waitress promptly replied, "We're only selling slow ones today." I thought that was funny. At another time, my husband had taken me out to eat and when we had finished the meal, the waitress appeared and said, "Your check, sir." He just looked up at her and with a very straight face, asked, "If I sign that check will you cash it?"

Likewise, why do we part in the driveway and speed on the parkway? Why do women get a permanent every six months if it is supposed to be permanent? And have you ever wondered why your nose runs and your feet smell? A few years ago, a restaurant had a sign on the window that said, "Eight pieces of chicken. Four free biscuits." The sign read exactly that way. I found it quite humorous so pulling up to the drive-thru window I calmly said, "I don't want any chicken, but I'll take the four free biscuits." It turned out the manager was the one at the window and this poor man had no sense of humor at all. But the next day I noticed the sign read, "Buy eight pieces of chicken for $5.99 and get four free biscuits."

Just the other day I was in a store and the cashier was wearing a button that advertised the name of the store and directly under it was the sentence, "It's your store." When she told me the total of my purchase I ask why I had to pay for it and with a puzzled look on her face she explained, "Because you're buying it."

"But your button says it's *my* store. You mean I must pay for something that already belongs to me?" This lady had no sense of humor either.

It's our crazy mixed up language. Our words alone send the wrong messages. Maybe it's the pollution in the air and it causes our hearing and understanding to malfunction. Anyway, to explain how the messages travel....

The body is composed of cells. Among all the cells are nerve cells. The nerve cells conduct electricity and communicate or talk to each other. Sorta like a Christian in need and relating this to other Christians. It is through this communication we construct our experiences.

This communication system is built from billions of cells that are interconnected. These cells are called neurons. To understand what I'm trying to convey, form a mental image of the body being a system with the brain as the circuit board.

With the brain being the circuit board that leaves the cranial nerves being the main system and branching out from this is a composite of subsystems and these in turn branch out to even smaller systems. It's like me going to an ATM (small system) and doing a transaction, then the ATM relays it to the next system all the way up the line.

Have you ever watched someone construct a house? Each part in itself is simplicity but once it's all together, it's complex. (At least to those of us that don't know how to construct houses.) But in the body the building blocks are actually the neurons, the cells that connect the communication system together.

Nerves work by sending impulses or commands to the parts of the body that is to be used. It is these neurons *talking* with other neurons that form the body's primary information center, or the nervous system. All the information passed along is bundled into the nerves like electrical cables. All of this is in the physical sense. So how does it tie in with the spiritual sense?

As I stated earlier, the twelve cranial nerves are in pairs making it a total of 24. They arise from the lower surface of the brain one on each side and pass through openings in the skull to the periphery of the body. There are twelve on each side with the right side sending messages to the left and the left sending messages to the right.

To me, this is very important. In the Body of Christ, this concept alone leaves no room for division with the Body. Physically, if the right side of the brain suffered a stroke, the left side would be affected. You see, basically, there's nothing wrong with the left side from the neck down but it is heavily damaged from the circuit board on the right side and the circuit board controls the body.

Spiritually? Look at Galatians 6:1. It reads, "Brethren, if man be overtaken in a fault, ye which are spiritual, restore such a one in the spirit of meekness; considering thyself, lest thou also be tempted."

It has been my experience to find very few who are willing to do this. In the body we have a tendency to point fingers, judge, scorn and ridicule our left side for being damaged, all the while forgetting that it's the right side that has the problem. When we see someone overtaken and damaged, we should ask ourselves how many times have we really prayed for that person? How many times have we fasted and sought God's face in his or her behalf and lifted them up and helped carry their burdens? So not only can we say as in Galatians 6:1 we could possibly suffer the same fate if we do not restore the damaged brother, but there's a possibility that we allowed it to happen by not interceding to God on his behalf.

Most of us have sense enough to know that if you invite someone to dinner and that someone has a cholesterol problem, you don't serve him or her fatty food. You go out of your way to prepare a wholesome, nutritious meal. It's called preventive care. So why don't we practice preventive care spiritually? Why don't we intercede in prayer whether our brother or sister is in need at that time or not? The nerves are the Body's communication system or vessels for prayer.

In studying the twelve cranial nerves, only to learn they are in pairs for a total of twenty-four, I suffered a lot of frustration. Not in the research but in wondering if I'd embarked on a journey that had no end...one of those mysteries we'll never know until we get to heaven. But as I said, God gave me the help I needed. The number twenty-four stands for the priesthood and in learning that, I was able to change my course in another direction. Let's look at the cranial nerves and their functions first.

Olfactory—of or relating to the sense of smell. This nerve is not highly developed in man and I believe it is because most of us have a tendency to smell the stink instead of the sweet fragrance of unity. Our sinuses can get so clogged that way.

Optic—of or relating to vision. This is interesting because as it turns out, these nerves are not really nerves at all, but should be thought of as a brain tract that's been drawn out from the cerebrum. The cerebrum is the expanded anterior or upper part of the brain that overlies the rest of the brain, and is considered to be the seat of conscious mental process. The reason this fascinated me was the nerves send messages to the body and the body acts upon what it receives. If the motor cortex sends a message through the nerve and tells your body to walk, it will respond by moving toward the desired object. But the optic is not really a nerve so how can we see the desired object if there is not a true nerve to carry the message? The optic is a tract and a tract, according to Webster is a bundle of nerve fibers having a common origin, termination, and function. The common origin and termination is Christ because He is the beginning and the end (Rev. 1:8) and the function is to aid you in walking by faith and not by actual sight.

Oculomotor—chiefly motor nerves arising from the mid brain and supplying four muscles of the eye. Complete division of this nerve can result in several visual problems. That's why we need to use it spiritually to direct our focus on spiritual matters.

Trochlear—the most slender of the cranial nerves and supplies only one muscle of the eye with motor fibers. It is held to resemble pulleys. This would relate spiritually to what Jesus told the disciples in John 16:8 concerning the duties of the Holy Ghost in that He was to reprove the world of sin. Remember this nerve resembles a pulley and a pulley is used to change the direction and point of application of the opposite pulling force.

Trigeminal—this nerve consists of three divisions supplying sensory fibers to the greater part of the skin of the head and face, the mucous membranes of the mouth, nose and paranasal air sinuses. In other words, it helps you feel when a sneeze is coming on.

Abducent—the motor nerves supplying the rectus or straight muscles on the outer and lateral side of each eye. Like the trochlear nerve, it supplies only one eye muscle. It is frequently involved in injuries to the base of the skull, giving rise to a convergent squint. Ever been so burdened that you had to squint to focus on the Problem Solver?

Facial—supplies muscles of facial expressions and motor fibers, especially to the muscles of the face and jaw and send a separate mixed branch to the tongue. I like this. Have you ever heard any one say, "Smile a while and give your face a rest?" It's because it takes a whole lot more muscles to frown than it does to smile. Frowning is work overload.

Auditory—connects the inner ear with the brain and transmits impulses concerned with hearing and balance. It consists of two sets of fibers: the cochlear, which is concerned with hearing and the vestibular, which is concerned with equilibrium. Remember the section on balance? Romans 10:17 says, "…faith cometh by hearing (or the cochlear) and hearing by the Word (or the vestibular, balance)."

Glossopharyngeal—contains sensory fibers for the pharynx (throat) and the bottom one third of the tongue. Damage to this can result in loss of taste and common sensation over the bottom of the tongue and some throat weakness. Most Christians who have this problem spiritually will loose their zeal to read the word and speak of Christ.

Vagus—has the most extensive distribution of all the cranial nerves affecting the heart and the major parts of the respiratory and alimentary tracts or nourishment. This is also called the wondering nerve.

Accessory—comprises a small cranial root, which is distributed by way of the vagus to the muscles of the palate, throat and a larger spinal root.

Hypoglossal—supplies intrinsic or extrinsic muscles of the tongue. Divisions involving its nucleus result in a wasting of the muscles of the tongue. Frankly, I've met some who could stand a little division of the nucleus of the hypoglossal.

Now you've been introduced to the cranial nerves and we've found there are twenty-four and twenty-four stands for priesthood. Each nerve has a specific function. So how does all this represent priesthood?

Consider the location. These nerves (representing man's position in the Lord) arise from the lower part of the brain (with the brain representing the Father, Son and Holy Spirit) and extend through the opening in the skull. When man was created we had a direct channel to God…face to face.

That channel was broken when man sinned. There had to be an atonement, a blood sacrifice, since the life was in the blood, to reconcile man with God. The animal sacrifices would only cover the sin and hide it. It never washed it away. With Christ we are washed and cleansed. However, the prophets and patriarchs of old, even though they offered sacrifices, still looked forward to the coming of the ultimate sacrifice, Jesus the Christ. The animal sacrifice was man's way of reaching up to God. The sacrifice of Jesus was God's way of reaching down to man.

The best explanation I could find in the Bible of a high priest was in Hebrews 5:1. "For every high priest taken from among men is ordained for men in things pertaining to God, that he may offer both gifts and sacrifices for sins." The high priest of Old Testament days, the first being Aaron, would approach God in the people's behalf, offering sacrifices and intercession for them. Likewise, he would also represent God to the people instructing them about God and His law.

Before the Law, the family head performed the duties of a priest and in the event of the father's death that duty would pass to the eldest son who offered sacrifice and intercession for his children. The family head must have acted as priests to their offspring until the Levitical Law and priesthood was ordained of God because when He brought the people to Mount Sinai He gave this command: "And let the priests also which come near the Lord, sanctify themselves, lest the Lord break forth upon them."

And this was said *before* the Law was given. God promised Israel they would become 'a kingdom of priests and a holy nation' if they would keep His covenant. (Exodus 19:6) And this priesthood would last until the coming of the One it foreshadowed which was the greater priesthood of Jesus Christ. (Hebrews 8:4-7)

"But how does this tie in with the cranial nerves?" you're probably asking by now. I'm headed that way so bear with me.

In a previous chapter we spoke of the protection for the brain, which is the skull, being in itself a representative of Christ because of the matching components of calcium, also being found in rock, with Christ being the Rock. By the cranial nerves being located at the lower surface of the brain and extending through the skull to the body, we see a perfect picture of us having to go through Jesus to be reconciled to God. He is our High Priest.

In the communication system of our physical body, the nerves are equipped with two things. First are the sensory fibers that carry messages *to* the brain from the tissues and organs. This is a priest making intercession for us. Second are the motor fibers that carry messages *from* the brain to tissues and organs. Works like this: Sensory fibers sends message saying, "I just got burned real bad." The motor fibers send back a message that says, "So?...scream."

On the day of Pentecost the Law covenant was completed and the new covenant was instated. Peter told the people that day as he rose to preach, that from that day forward their salvation lay in the acceptance of Jesus alone. Later, in I Peter 2:9 he wrote, "But ye are a chosen generation, a royal priesthood, a holy nation, a peculiar people, they ye should show forth the praises of him who hath called you out of darkness into this marvelous light."

Under the Levitical Law only the High Priest could enter the Holy of Holies. But by our acceptance of Christ and Him becoming our High Priest, we may now enter the Holy of Holies ourselves and boldly approach the Throne of Grace. (Hebrews 4:16. How can we do this when you were just told that only the High Priest could enter? It's because of the vanity of the law. Remember? The animal sacrifices only covered our sins. Christ's blood completely washes them away.

One last thought and then I'll let you go eat your dinner. Something I find quite amazing is that all the cranial nerves have one thing in common and of course, that is their location. The only other note of special interest is that all these nerves relay messages to parts of the head but one. That particular one, the vagus, supplies the heart and major parts of the respiratory and alimentary tracts. Does anything leap right out at you here?

Eleven of these nerves are fleshly things that we in ourselves can do without. You always hear of people that have lost their hearing, or their taste buds not doing the job, or even their ability to smell. And with all this, they still lead almost perfectly normal lives. There are bodily functions we can do without. But the one that feeds messages to our heart (the seat of our affection); the respiratory system (where the life entered the blood); and our alimentary, or nourishment tract (where we grow by eating the Word) is the one in which its absence would leave us dead. And to beat it all, that nerve is the tenth one...and the number ten stands for the law, my friend.

15

Have We Been Decapitated?

How many of you have ever seen a chicken after someone cuts off its head? It's a nasty sight. I remember my dad did this once. We had some chickens and he decided he wanted one for dinner. So I followed him outside and down the path to the chicken coup. After looking them over, he singled one out, grabbed it and after getting the chicken positioned the way he wanted, promptly and with one swift swing of the ax, dislocated its head from its body. He let it fall on the ground, and I thought that was the end of it. But to my horror, the chicken continued to wiggle, flop and move around for quite a long time.

Ever heard the expression 'running around like a chicken with its head cut off'? It's disgusting. My dad said it was just muscle spasms (like I knew what that was at that age) and it would stop shortly but it made me have second thoughts about that chicken when mom put it on the table that night. Somehow it had lost its appeal. I kept expecting it to get up and run. I just knew that when I bit into that drumstick, it would cluck. It made me completely lose my appetite and my mother, being the person she was, decided I was very ill and needed a doctor. The doctor decided she was over reacting and said I probably had a virus.

Now the standard joke of today is when a doctor says you have a virus, it really means he doesn't know what's wrong. But the bad part of it was, my mother believed him and made me stay in bed all the next day. All because a hyperactive chicken didn't know when to give up and die. During those days, freedom of expression was unheard of and you didn't talk back to your mother and tell her the chicken wasn't dead when she tried to make you eat it, never mind the fact that you would probably be laughed at and made to feel like a total idiot. But that just proves the point of how some things can give the appearance of life, when it is actually not even breathing. And this little illustration can be used to show how the Body is responding today. So what do you say to us taking a step to no longer being the chicken and giving the appearance of being alive and show the world that we really are?

The Body is flopping around and from all practical purposes is giving the world the appearance that our Head has been cut off. And the sad part is we have lived this way so long we don't even realize it. Why is there so much dissension among the cells? Why are we struggling to gain victory over things that were taken care of at Calvary? Why do we seek deliverance from the sins that so easily beset us and it always seems like it's an inch from our grasp? Why does it seem like we pray and pray and there never is an answer?

First, let's remember who we are. We are sons and daughters of the Most Holy God. Christ is the only begotten Son of God and we are adopted into the family. Since He is God's Son and we are God's adopted children, that makes Him our big brother.

We are also joint heirs with Him. If we are joint heirs that means we have access to every thing God owns and He owns it all. He has put everything at our disposal and still we struggle and whine and harbor fear. We have listened to a defeated tongue so long we have accepted it.

Secondly, we need to realize the authority we have. Oh, we say all the time we can do anything in Christ Jesus but we don't believe it. We say our battles were won at Calvary but we don't believe it. You can prove we don't believe it because of our actions. Always having a Plan B, and when God does answer our prayers we're always amazed. We should always be thankful but have the attitude of, "I've been expecting this."

One thing I've learned is I'm a child of God and I don't have to take this. If I'm doing what I'm supposed to be doing then I've got a right to say, "Bug off Satan."

One of the problems with the Body can be compared to Judges 17:6 and Judges 21:25. In both of these verses it says there was no king in those days and everyone did that which was right in his own eyes. They had prophets and judges but that wasn't enough for them. Samuel was a major prophet of those days and when he was getting old, he made his sons judges over Israel. However his sons did not walk in the ways of the Lord. We find the account of this in I Samuel 8.

Read this passage carefully and see how the people conducted themselves. Let's look at it together.

The people had judges and prophets, of which Samuel was one. Everyone did what he wanted to do. Sorta like the phrase that was going around a few years ago, "If it feels good, do it."

But at the same time they really weren't happy, they wanted more. They knew the law of God but it wasn't what they wanted. Have you ever paid attention to how the Body of today is trying to justify everything we do? People are getting away with breaking the law based on how they were treated as a child. They were abused, they were neglected, they were abandoned, they were made to clean their room and eat their spinach, do their homework and go to bed at a deceit hour. So sad, so sad.

Even after Samuel told them what it would be like to have a king they still wanted one. When Samuel consulted with the Lord on the matter, God told him to go ahead because they hadn't rejected Samuel by wanting a king, they had rejected Him. They wanted a Head, but they wanted to choose which one. They wanted a ruler, but not God or His judges or His prophets.

When God created the earth He gave dominion to mankind. Dominion means to rule in a particular domain. The earth is our domain. God gave us the authority over everything on this earth. The animals, the plants, the fowls of the air, even the elements such as the wind and rain. The only thing He did not give us dominion over was each other. That's why it was wrong when they wanted a king. God had already told them how to live but they wanted no part of it. God had already told them they had dominion but they wanted no part of it.

Adam gave up the right to rule when he sinned and this allowed the devil to have control of this domain. God wants us to take it back. He gave us Jesus so we would have the power to do just that. You must understand that God is a Spirit and when He made us in His image He made us a spirit. He then installed that spirit in a body. Our mind is the soul or the link of communication to the spiritual realm.

Jesus told the disciples that whatever we bind on earth shall be bound in heaven and whatever we loose on earth shall be loosed in heaven. (Matthew 18:18)

Whatever we do on earth is also taking place in heaven. If we bind the problem here, it is bound in heaven first. If we overcome here it is done in heaven first.

Satan is the ruler of this present world now. He is the prince of this world. The Body, if It responds to the messages the Head sends, can still have that power. One day it will be the way God wanted it to be in the first place, with the people in unison. But for now, the Body is acting as though we have been decapitated. Take the authority in your own hands and speak to the problem. It is under your ruler-ship because of the work on Calvary. Speak to that mountain! It's not a blab it and grab it situation. It's not a name it and claim it situation. It is a simple thing of God wanting a place for the things in heaven to be manifested in the physical realm so He chose to put man in charge on earth. Adam blew it and the Body is trying to blow it again. Take charge. Take authority. And do this by letting the Head rule the Body or have you been decapitated?

0-595-35055-0

Books

THE Arithmetic of God — Don Kistler

THE Tongue, a creative Force — Charles Capp

CPSIA information can be obtained at www.ICGtesting.com
Printed in the USA
BVOW011733121112

305332BV00002B/95/A

9 780595 350551